TWENTIETH CENTURY VIEWS

The aim of this series is to present the best in contemporary critical opinion on major authors, providing a twentieth century perspective on their changing status in an era of profound revaluation.

Maynard Mack, *Series Editor*
Yale University

E M I L Y
DICKINSON

A COLLECTION OF CRITICAL ESSAYS

Edited by

Richard B. Sewall

A SPECTRUM BOOK

Prentice-Hall, Inc., *Englewood Cliffs, N. J.*

Examples of Emily Dickinson's poetry and letters taken from versions published in the three-volume complete edition of *The Poems of Emily Dickinson,* edited by Thomas H. Johnson, are reprinted by permission of The Trustees of Amherst College from Thomas H. Johnson, Editor, *The Poems of Emily Dickinson* and *The Letters of Emily Dickinson,* Cambridge, Mass., The Belknap Press, Harvard University Press, Copyright 1955, 1958 by the President and Fellows of Harvard College.

Permission has also been obtained from Little, Brown and Company, publishers of *The Complete Poems* of Emily Dickinson, Copyright 1914, 1929, 1935, 1942, © 1957, 1963, by Mary L. Hampson and Martha Dickinson Bianchi to quote poems of which Little, Brown is the original publisher. Additional permission has been granted by Houghton Mifflin Company, Boston, to reprint portions of Poems 1072 and 1454 of the Johnson edition published by Harvard University Press.

Current printing (last digit):

13   12   11   10   9   8   7   6   5   4

LIBRARY OF CONGRESS CATALOG CARD NO.: 63-9307

Printed in the United States of America

C 20878

Table of Contents

Introduction

by Richard B. Sewall

The theme of this anthology, to take a cue from Mr. Ransom's essay, is "A poet restored." Readers sensitive to chronology will note that nearly two-thirds of the essays in this volume were written during or since the year 1955. I like to think that this fact is not so much a matter of editorial taste as an objective indication of how recent the "restoration" has been. The year 1955 saw the publication of the Harvard edition of Emily Dickinson's poems under the editorship of Thomas H. Johnson. Sixty-nine years after the poet's death, this edition at last made available, in one place, all of her poems—finished, unfinished, fragmentary—printed with scrupulous regard to the manuscripts, and honoring all her choices of spelling, punctuation, capitalization and line and stanza division, even when these seemed eccentric. All her variant readings were printed, and an attempt was made, for the first time, to arrange the poems in chronological order. Those who know the troubled history of the publication of these poems—the Ransom and Warren essays give some account of it—realize how long and frustrating the wait has been. A glance at the "Chronology of Important Dates" at the end of this volume will show in what piecemeal fashion the poems have come to us. But what the "Chronology" does not show is that no edition until 1955 came within six hundred-odd poems of being "complete." There may be a few poems still outstanding, datings may change as new information comes to light, but, with decent allowance for possible new evidence, we now have the materials with which to see the great body of Emily Dickinson's poetry steadily and see it whole.

There has been nothing in our critical annals quite like the sense of discovery that animated the reviews and revaluations that greeted the new edition. When the Harvard edition of the *Letters* appeared in 1958, the acknowledgment that something momentous had happened was general. For the first time, scholars, critics, and readers could approach her with the sense that their response need not be tentative. The 1775 poems and the 1049 letters were the final embodiment of the hitherto fragmented sources of her readers' enthusiasm—an event much like the publication that crowns a living writer's career.

This is not to say that nothing true or perceptive had been written

1

about her before 1955. Historically, the present "restoration" is the latest of at least four flurries of interest in her work, each one with its appropriate occasion. The first was in the 1890's when the posthumous publication of three slim volumes of her verse (1890, '91, '96) met with decided popular but little critical success. The second began in 1914, accompanying a series of publications by her niece, Martha Dickinson Bianchi (see "Chronology"). The third came in 1945 with the publication of *Bolts of Melody*. This volume indicated the inadequate basis of previous summings-up, set new standards of editorial precision, and whetted the general appetite for a complete, definitive edition. It was the harbinger of the "restoration," and its Introduction is required reading on the problem of deciphering the manuscripts. If the present anthology contains only one essay published before 1930, it is because the preoccupation till then had been largely biographical and the criticism fragmentary. Aiken (with whose historically important essay of 1924 this anthology begins) and Tate were among the first to take Emily Dickinson seriously as a poet. Winters' astringent criticism was a welcome antidote to misplaced unction, and the title of Whicher's book was properly admonitory: *This Was a Poet,* a phrase taken from one of her own poems, where the important issue had lain all along. Whicher's book, the first full-length attempt at a critical and biographical estimate, though now superseded, was a triumph when one considers the incomplete and fragmentary state of the materials at his disposal. Henry Wells' *Introduction to Emily Dickinson* (1947) extended the critical study of her diction, form, and major themes. Donald Thackrey's essay is a brilliant bit of "pre-restoration" textual criticism. But events of the mid- and late fifties demanded further and fresh treatment.

If the restoration brought a new text, new letters, a chronology that provided at least a working basis for discussion, and a host of new peripheral, and some central, data, what has been the discernible effect on our attitude toward her as person and poet?

In the area of biographical studies, Millicent Todd Bingham's thorough documentation in *Emily Dickinson's Home,* which appeared in 1955, shed a flood of new light on Emily's family relationships, home-life, and friends. Mrs. Bingham's central chapters are justly commended in Mr. Warren's essay. I would only single out, for the benefit of those who still see Emily Dickinson as the Moth of Amherst, "meditating," in Jay Leyda's parody of the romantic notion of her, "majestically among her flowers," the short chapter called "The Making of a Home," where we see the poet, with conclusive immediacy, busily involved in a very work-a-day world. Thomas Johnson's "interpretive biography" of that same year synthesized much of the new material. In 1960, Leyda expanded the scholarly and factual approach to the biographical problem with his two-volume chronology, *The Years and Hours of Emily Dickinson.* What Leyda has called the "late thaw of a frozen image" was complete.

Textually, the 1955 variorum edition opened a new era. No poet had ever suffered more from the vicissitudes of editing. (It was her own fault; she never prepared her poems for publication.) The new edition made a vital difference in several ways. First, we can now see her *developmentally,* though only broadly so, since the dating of the poems is only approximate. There are still mysteries—for instance, the different phases of her career cannot all be neatly articulated—but we can get a panoramic view of her work as never before. The early poems, those which in the editions of a standard poet would have been, from the first, tucked away in "juvenilia," can now be seen as such. Though Mr. Warren may be right in saying that she never entirely outgrew any of her styles, I venture to say that future studies will discern modulations of tone and rhetoric impossible to trace in the old editions.

Second, the wealth of variants, often half a dozen for as many lines, sometimes for one line, reveal at a glance how many poems had been published in earlier editions as if completed to her satisfaction. Of these variants, it is often impossible to determine Emily Dickinson's own choice, and hence editorial choice may be arbitrary. We can also see how many of the poems first appeared in letters or were quoted in them in whole or in part—the only form of publication she seems to have enjoyed. We are thus constantly reminded of the occasional nature of many of the poems. It is not that they were dashed off and are hence forgivable. But the *jeux d'esprit,* the congratulatory or consolatory bits, too often appearing in earlier editions as solemn parts of what she called her "letter to the world," can now be properly seen as personal parts of dialogues, occasions quite *à deux.*

Then there is her ubiquitous and eccentric form of punctuation—the dash. The Harvard edition was the first to attempt a typographical approximation of the curious Dickinson pointing, and it has been a matter of concern to almost all post-1955 commentators. The attempt was necessarily an approximation, for the manuscripts show how varied her use of the dash was—long, short, high, low, slanting up, slanting down. There was sufficient uniformity in the manuscripts, nevertheless, to warrant the attempt. After recovering from the initial shock, many students of her work agree that it was justified and that there should be no retreat. Mr. Warren's suggestion that in future editions all punctuation except periods be omitted would, if adopted, do violence to what now seems to be a clear and indisputable fact of the Dickinson idiom. Rightly or wrongly, this is the way she envisaged her poems. She could not have used the dashes so often, throughout so much of her career, unless she meant them. Had she published her poems and listened to her editors, she would most probably have modified her procedure, at least to some extent; but this is what we have from her hand, and there seems less point in changing it than in leaving it as she wrote it. The technique is true to her idiom, to the way she thought—tentatively, a little breathlessly. It is also true to her

amateurism, a constant reminder that she was not a publishing poet and
that she indulged her amateur's idiosyncrasy to the full. There is something *to the life* about her waywardness. The "well-made" syntax of
some of the poems in earlier edited versions (or, even, in some post-1955
anthologies which attempt to conventionalize her habits) seems tame
and sedate by comparison.

What has been the restoration's effect in criticism? With its new perspective, the criticism from 1955 on has been freer of the old tone of
grudgingness and apology on the one hand and fulsomeness and cloying
unction on the other. There is now little dispute about her stature—we
can hardly miss its dimensions—and, given the size of her achievement,
there is less inclination to complain about her unevenness. We accept the
fact that she wrote much that was not up to her best, like all poets. There
is even a belated recognition, as Reeves and Bogan point out, that there
is something valuable in having *all* of a poet before us, the rough drafts,
the scraps, the variants. There is not so much fussing over her girlishness
and her obvious failures, not so many exclamations of "How can you call
that the work of a great poet?" We can take some of these old responses
more in stride and refrain from blaming the poet, as we sometimes used
to do, for our lack of poise when confronted by the necessity of distinguishing between her good and bad work.

Mr. Blackmur finds his own critical estimate unchanged. He says he
finds "nothing . . . that would make me alter the judgment I found
rising from the reading of the poems twenty years ago . . ." This reaction
is not typical of the other essays, however, and even in the case of Mr.
Blackmur, there is a marked difference in tone between his essay of 1938
(for which Mr. Reeves takes him somewhat ungently to task) and the
1957 essay printed here. As Reeves says, Blackmur's (and I might add
Winters') early scepticisms came at a time when adulation of Emily
Dickinson tended to the cultish.

Of the effects on criticism, perhaps the most important is that the new
edition has encouraged textual studies of a thoroughness and variety that
the earlier state of the Dickinson canon made impossible. Though the
Explicator magazine has, it is true, printed analyses of many poems since
1943, a full-length study such as Charles R. Anderson's *Stairway of
Surprise* (1960), where a hundred-odd poems are discussed in detail,
would not have been feasible until the Harvard edition. Again, it was
Johnson's biography of 1955 that first analyzed thoroughly Emily Dickinson's use of hymn meters. Reeves is now permitted close-up examination
of peculiarities of syntax, meter, and diction, and after it is able to cap a
decades-old debate with the salutary reminder: "We have to do with a
poet of almost total originality, and it is very rarely that originality and
formal perfection go together." MacLeish defines her tone—her "voice"
—with great sensitivity and can point precisely to the ways in which she
achieves it. The essays by Wilbur and Bogan (with MacLeish's, two of

the distinguished contributions to the Bicentennial celebration of the Town of Amherst, on October 23, 1959) can deal with large thematic matters in a more comprehensive way than the old, incomplete editions allowed.

"It is finished," Emily Dickinson once wrote, "can never be said of us." It certainly cannot be said of her. The circle of her affinities continues to grow, from Tate's efforts to place her in the setting of nineteenth-century America to Miss Bogan's discussion of her kinship with the tradition of mystical poetry. She is variously a mystical poet, a romantic poet, a Metaphysical, a Transcendentalist, and, most recently, a Meditative poet. And there is much new material, in Leyda's two-volume chronology and elsewhere, that needs to be woven into the fabric of her biography and from there, so powerful is the sense of personal involvement her poetry gives, into the poems. The editor of this volume can only offer, at this point, a few parting caveats.

First, as to the biographical problem. In spite of the wealth of new material made available in the last decade, it still *is* a problem. The situation is not a little Shakespearean: how could the country boy from Stratford have written such plays? We look for sources in her external life to account for the rich and vivid life of the poems and find ourselves frustrated at almost every turn. Hence the perennial pursuit of "the lover," or the tendency to make of a single figure like her father the center around which her entire life revolved. The most sensible short statement about Emily's affairs of passion appears in Mrs. Bingham's *Emily Dickinson, A Revelation*: "It was Emily's way to form extravagant attachments. She needed an object of devotion and poured out her love on her friends . . . These youthful friendships [one of her teachers, Elizabeth Adams; Jane Humphrey, Susan Gilbert, Leonard Humphrey, Benjamin Newton, Vaughan Emmons, John Graves] were followed by a succession of deep lasting attachments [Rev. Charles Wadsworth, Samuel Bowles, Judge Otis Lord] . . . Each was to Emily profoundly revealing. Each brought its own special insight, different from that of any other, and all were fervently cherished . . . It cannot be said too emphatically or too often that Emily Dickinson's understanding of the human heart is not to be explained in terms of any one person." The warning to the reader of the present volume is clear. Many of our essayists, following a long-standing tradition, have assumed that Emily's life was broken in two by the Rev. Charles Wadsworth of Philadelphia. We know that she met the man, that he called on her twice in Amherst, that she wrote letters to him and revered him. That is all. As Mrs. Bingham points out, she had other friends just as vital, perhaps more so, and one final, documented relationship as near to a love affair as any attachment of her life—with Judge Lord of Salem. Beyond that, everything is speculation.

Another caveat regards the chronology of the poems. Beware the spinning of theories involving a too precise dating of the poems. In general, though not always, it is true that we can tell the early ones from the later, but the handwriting is not an infallible clue. For instance, we know that there are some six hundred poems in the handwriting of the late fifties and early sixties, suggesting for those years a prodigious poetic output. Since many of them are anguished or in some way expressive of deep trouble, and since many of the letters of that period suggest emotional disturbance, we assume that this outpouring of poetry was occasioned by some great emotional disaster, like the failure of a love affair. But there is no proof that all the poems written in the handwriting of this period were composed then. Indeed, she might merely have chosen this time to make fresh copies of old poems whose composition might well have dated a decade back. It is hard to believe that she suddenly emerged as a full-fledged poet at the age of 27 or 28; yet this is the time, save for a few obvious juvenilia like the Valentines, at which the Harvard edition begins to date the poems. To be sure, in light of all available evidence, such a dating was the only proper course, and the date printed after every poem is preceded by a saving "about." But no biographical theory can rest its claim of authority on this chronology. Although the most delicate and sensitive of the theorists, Theodora Ward (*Capsule of the Mind,* 1962), follows, in general, the Harvard chronology, which she herself helped devise, she is thoroughly aware of what she is doing. The reader is never in doubt about the speculative nature of the sequence in which she puts the poems to fill out the story she sees them telling, and the resulting insight into what is happening in the poems and *might have happened* in Emily Dickinson's mind and heart is extremely illuminating. Such speculation is legitimate and profitable as long as it is not confused with absolute historical truth, especially when this truth bears, as it does, so problematical a relationship to an artist's life as artist. If the emotional crisis which is so often associated with Emily Dickinson's flood of creativity were of a severity equal to the greatness of the poetry, one wonders how she could have found strength to put pen to paper or mind to matter. This kind of one-to-one correspondence between life and art is highly questionable. It is well-known that some artists—Mozart, for example—have written some of their most joyous work in their blackest moments and some of their most somber work in their lightest moments. The production of a masterpiece must require a fund of psychic energy so deep as to be ill-provided by a sensibility exhausted by personal passions, at least while these are raging at their highest.

Another parting caveat, or series of them, is perhaps gratuitous but irresistible. In spite of their large agreement on Emily Dickinson's stature, our essayists disagree on details, and the editor (as I hope the reader) finds himself frequently in the thick of it. For instance: I cannot agree with Winters that the poem "I like to see it lap the miles" is "abominable," an example of her "silly playfulness." It is playful perhaps, but not silly. And what is "barbaric" about the fourth line of the poem beginning " 'Twas warm at first, like us"?

Again: Ransom misreads, I think, "At half past three a single bird." He has the poem covering a span of sixteen hours instead of what seems only four, the morning chorus that greets the sun subsiding when the sun is fully risen, a reading further supported by the poem, "The Birds begun at Four o'clock." And Blackmur: what is so "immature," even within his special definition of that word, about "Rearrange a wife's affections"? It is the fact of control that I would say constitutes the poem's particular grandeur. And I see little point in his rearrangement of "Much Madness is divinest Sense," as if he were demonstrating a universal truth about Emily Dickinson's poems, whereas he is really saying that this particular poem *could* work the other way. It seems clear, however, that it works better her way and that, though not among her best, it is not without distinction.

On larger issues, too, I find myself prone to debate. Ransom predicted that only one out of seventeen of her poems would "become a common public property." As the literature on Emily Dickinson's poetry mounts, it is clear that readers are pressing far beyond the few dozen favorites of the past and making many more poems their own. She is a "popular poet," and her popularily is not to be measured by the traditional anthology pieces. T. S. Eliot has reminded us that a knowledge of the whole of a major poet's work alters our view of every single part. What Winters called "the desert of her crudities" is yielding many riches. Again: how can Blackmur say that "she married herself," that she was all "withdrawal" and no "return," in the face of her brilliantly objective and concrete nature poetry and her many psychological, philosophic, and semantic analyses, so perceptive of purely external fact as to be all but academic and clinical? Having led, quite consciously, a metaphorical life, Emily Dickinson is often the cause of metaphor in her commentators. I would gently warn against it.

So our discussion goes, and should go, as more and more truth emerges from the press of dialectic and taste. It all points to one large conclusion: that we still are not quite sure of her. We ask and ask. The image of almost every other major lyric poet is by comparison fixed and certain. Teachers send their students to Donne and Yeats and Frost with an assurance (justified or otherwise) not yet applicable to Emily Dickinson. We do not quite trust ourselves, and the apologetic note persists. I said before that there is now no doubt that her poetry has stature. But what are its true dimensions and what is its specific nature? The latest phase of her restoration has taken us a long way, but there are hundreds of poems still left to explicate, and there are many dimensions of her life and personality that are still indistinct or ill-assimilated in the public vision. Perhaps we shall all be better off when we resist completely the temptation to condescend to her. We have not yet taken seriously Mr. Tate's advice of thirty years ago: "All pity for Miss Dickinson's 'starved life' is misdirected. Her life was one of the richest and deepest ever lived on this continent." My own prediction is that Emily Dickinson will grow stronger with the years as we continue to outdistance the sentimentalities that still cling to her. Her eccentricities will fall into perspective. We will become increasingly aware of the toughness and sinew of her poetry, its range and versatility, its challenge to our understanding. We will test our knowledge of humanity against hers and find that we can learn on almost every front. Far from the little figure of frustrations and renunciations and regrets, we will come to see her as a poet of great strength, courage, and singleness of purpose.

A Note on the Texts of the Poems

All poems quoted in essays written before the publication of the variorum edition of 1955 use texts based on earlier editions listed in the Chronology of Important Dates.

Emily Dickinson

by Conrad Aiken

Emily Dickinson was born in Amherst, Massachusetts, on December 10, 1830. She died there, after a life perfectly devoid of outward event, in 1886. She was thus an exact contemporary of Christina Rossetti, who was born five days earlier than she, and outlived her by eight years. Of her life we know little. Her father, Edward Dickinson, was a lawyer, and the Treasurer of Amherst College; and it is clear that what social or intellectual life was in that bleak era available, was available for her. That she did not choose to avail herself of it, except in very slight degree, is also clear; and that this choice, which was gradually to make of her life an almost inviolable solitude, was made early, is evident from her Letters. In a letter dated 1853, when she was twenty-three years old, she remarked, "I do not go from home." By the time she was thirty, the habit of sequestration had become distinct, a subject on which she was explicit and emphatic in her letters to T. W. Higginson—essayist and contributor to the *Atlantic Monthly* at that time. She made it clear that if there was to be any question of a meeting between them, he would have to come to Amherst—she would not go to Boston. Higginson, as a matter of fact, saw her twice, and his record of the encounter is practically the only record we have of her from any "literary" personage of her lifetime. Even this is meager—Higginson saw her superficially, as was inevitable. Brave soldier, courtly gentleman, gifted amateur of letters, he was too much of the old school not to be a little puzzled by her poetry; and if he was fine enough to guess the fineness, he was not quite fine enough wholly to understand it. The brief correspondence between these two is an extraordinary document of unconscious irony—the urbanely academic essayist reproaching his wayward pupil for her literary insubordination, her false quantities, and reckless liberties with rhyme; the wayward pupil replying with a humility, beautiful and pathetic, but remaining singularly, with unmalleable obstinacy, herself. "I saw her," wrote Higginson, "but twice, face to face, and brought away the impression of something as unique and remote as Undine or Mignon or Thekla." When, thirty years after the acquaintance had begun, and four after Emily Dickinson's death, he was asked for assistance and advice in making a selection from her poetry, practically none of which had been published during her lifetime, his scruples were less severe, and he spoke of her with generosity and insight. "After all," he then wrote, "when a thought takes one's breath away, a lesson on grammar seems an impertinence." Again, "In many cases these verses will seem to the reader like poetry torn up by the roots." And again, "a quality more suggestive of the poetry of Blake than of anything to be elsewhere found—flashes of wholly original and profound insight into nature and life."

Thus began and ended Emily Dickinson's only important connection with the literary life of her time. She knew, it is true, Helen Hunt Jackson, a poetess, for whose anthology, *A Masque of Poets,* she gave the poem "Success," one of the few poems she allowed publication during her life. And she knew the Bowles family, owners and editors of the *Springfield Republican,* at that time the *Manchester Guardian* of New England—which, as she put it mischievously, was one of "such papers . . . as have nothing carnal in them." But these she seldom saw; and aside from these she had few intimates outside of her family; the circle of her world grew steadily smaller. This is a point of cardinal importance, but unfortunately no light has been thrown upon it. It is apparent that Miss Dickinson became a hermit by deliberate and conscious choice. "A recluse," wrote Higginson, "by temperament and habit, literally spending years without setting her foot beyond the doorstep, and many more years during which her walks were strictly limited to her father's grounds, she habitually concealed her mind, like her person, from all but a very few friends; and it was with great difficulty that she was persuaded to print, during her lifetime, three or four poems." One of the co-editors of Poems: Second Series assures us that this voluntary hermitage was not due to any "love-disappointment," and that she was "not an invalid." "She had tried society and the world, and had found them lacking." But this, of course, tells us nothing. Her Letters show us convincingly that her girlhood was a normally "social" one—she was active, high-spirited, and endowed with a considerable gift for extravagant humor. As a young woman she had, so Mrs. Bianchi, a niece, informed us in the preface to *The Single Hound,* several "love-affairs," but there is no evidence that any of them was serious, and we have no right, without other testimony, to assume here any ground for the singular psychological change that came over her. The only other clue we have, of any sort, is the hint from one of her girlhood friends, that, perhaps, *"she was longing for poetic sympathy."* Perhaps! But this, too, tells us very little. Anecdotes relating to her mischievousness, her wit, her waywardness, are not enough.

It is amusing, if horrifying, to know that once, being anxious to dispose of some kittens, she put them on a shovel, carried them into the cellar, and dropped them into the nearest jar—which, subsequently, on the occasion of the visit of a distinguished judge, turned out to have been the pickle-jar. We like to know, too, that even when her solitude was most remote she was in the habit of lowering from her window, by a string, small baskets of fruit or confectionery for children. But there are other things we should like to know much more.

There seems now, however, little likelihood of our ever learning anything more; and if we seek for the causes of the psychic injury which so sharply turned her in upon herself, we can only speculate. Her letters, in this regard, give little light, only showing us again and again that the injury was deep. Of the fact that she suffered acutely from intellectual drought, there is evidence enough. One sees her vividly here—but one sees her, as it were, perpetually in retreat; always discovering anew, with dismay, the intellectual limitations of her correspondents; she is discreet, pathetic, baffled, a little humbled, and draws in her horns; takes sometimes a perverse pleasure in indulging more than ever, on the occasion of such a disappointment, in her love of a cryptic style—a delicate bombardment of parable and whim which she perfectly knows will stagger; and then again retreats to the safe ground of the superficial. It is perhaps for this reason that the letters give us so remarkably little information about her literary interests. The meagerness of literary allusion is astounding. The Brontës and the Brownings are referred to—she thought Alexander Smith "not very coherent"—Joaquin Miller she "could not care about." Of her own work she speaks only in the brief unsatisfactory correspondence with Higginson. To him she wrote in 1863, "I wrote no verse, but one or two, until this winter." Otherwise, no scrap of her own literary history: she appears to have existed in a vacuum. Of the literary events, tremendous for America, which were taking place during her most impressionable years, there is hardly a mention. Emerson was at the height of his career, and living only sixty miles away: his poems came out when she was seventeen. When she was twenty, Hawthorne published *The Scarlet Letter,* and *The House of the Seven Gables* the year after. The same year, 1851, brought out Melville's *Moby Dick.* The death of Poe took place in 1849—in 1850 was published the first collected edition of his poems. When she was twenty-four, Thoreau's *Walden* appeared; when she was twenty-five, *Leaves of Grass.* One can say with justice that she came to full "consciousness" at the very moment when American literature came to flower. That she knew this, there cannot be any question; nor that she was stimulated and influenced by it. One must assume that she found in her immediate environment no one of her own stature, with whom she could admit or discuss such things; that she lacked the energy or effrontery to voyage out into the unknown in search of such companionship; and that lacking this courage, and wanting this help, she became easily a prey to the then current Emersonian doctrine of mystical individualism. In this connection it is permissible to suggest that her extreme self-seclusion and secrecy was both a protest and a display—a kind of vanity masquerading as modesty. She became increasingly precious, of her person as of her thought. Vanity is in her letters—at the last an unhealthy vanity. She believes that anything she says, however brief, will be of importance; however cryptic, will be deciphered. She enjoys being something of a mystery, and she sometimes deliberately and awkwardly exaggerates it. Even in notes of condolence—for which she had a morbid passion—she is vain enough to indulge in sententiousness: as when she wrote, to a friend whose father had died on her wedding-day, "Few daughters have the immortality of a father for a bridal gift."

When we come to Emily Dickinson's poetry, we find the Emersonian individualism clear enough, but perfectly Miss Dickinson's. Henry James observed of Emerson:

> The doctrine of the supremacy of the individual to himself, of his originality and, as regards his own character, *unique* quality, must have had a great charm for people living in a society in which introspection, thanks to the want of other entertainment, played almost the part of a social resource. . . . There was . . . much relish for the utterances of a writer who would help one to take a picturesque view of one's internal possibilities, and to find in the landscape of the soul all sorts of fine sunrise and moonlight effects.

This sums up admirably the social "case" of Miss Dickinson—it gives us a shrewd picture of the causes of her singular introversion, and it suggests that we are perhaps justified in considering her the most perfect flower of New England Transcendentalism. In her mode of life she carried the doctrine of self-sufficient individualism farther than Thoreau carried it, or the naïve zealots of Brook Farm. In her poetry she carried it, with its complement of passionate moral mysticism, farther than Emerson: which is to say that as a poet she had more genius than he. Like Emerson, whose essays must greatly have influenced her, and whose poetry, especially his gnomic poems, only a little less, she was from the outset, and remained all her life, a singular mixture of Puritan and free thinker. The problems of good and evil, of life and death, obsessed her; the nature and destiny of the human soul; and Emerson's theory of compensation. Toward God, as one of her earliest critics is reported to have said, "she exhibited an Emersonian self-possession." Indeed, she did not, and could not, accept the Puritan God at all. She was frankly irreverent, on occasion, a fact which seems to have made her editors a little uneasy—one hopes that it has not resulted in the suppression of any of her work. What she was irreverent to, of course, was the Puritan conception of God, the Puritan attitude toward Him. In "Drowning" she observes:

> The Maker's cordial visage,
> However good to see,
> Is shunned, we must admit it,
> Like an adversity.

In one poem she refers to God as "a noted clergyman" and on another occasion she salutes Him as "Burglar, banker, father"—a flippancy which might have annoyed even the most advanced of her contemporaries. But perhaps her perfect metaphysical detachment is most precisely and unabashedly stated in the famous mock-prayer (in "The Single Hound"), in which, addressing God, she quite impertinently apologizes to Him for His own "duplicity."

This, it must be repeated, is Emily Dickinson's opinion of the traditional and anthropomorphic "God," who was still, in her day, a portentous Victorian gentleman. Her real reverence, the reverence that made her a mystic poet of the finest sort, was reserved for Nature, which seemed to her a more manifest and more beautiful evidence of Divine Will than creeds and churches. This she saw, observed, loved, with a burning simplicity and passion which nevertheless did not exclude her very agile sense of humor. Her Nature poems, however, are not the most secretly revelatory or dramatically compulsive of her poems, nor, on the whole, the best. They are often of extraordinary delicacy—nearly always give us, with deft brevity, the exact in terms of the quaint. But, also, they are often superficial, a mere affectionate playing with the smaller things that give her delight; and to see her at her best and most characteristic and most profound, one must turn to the remarkable range of metaphysical speculation and ironic introspection which is displayed in those sections of her posthumous books which her editors have captioned Life, and Time and Eternity. In the former sections are the greater number of her set "meditations" on the nature of things. For some critics they will always appear too bare, bleak, and fragmentary. They have no trappings, only here and there a shred of purple. It is as if Miss Dickinson, who in one of her letters uttered her contempt for the "obtrusive body," had wanted to make them, as nearly as possible, disembodied thought. The thought is there, at all events, hard, bright, and clear; and her symbols, her metaphors, of which she could be prodigal, have an analogous clarity and translucency. What is also there is a downright homeliness which is a perpetual surprise and delight. Emerson's gnomic style she tunes up to the epigrammatic—the epigrammatic she often carries to the point of the cryptic; she becomes what one might call an epigrammatic symbolist.

> Lay this laurel on the one
> Too intrinsic for renown.
> Laurel! veil your deathless tree,—
> Him you chasten, that is he!

This, from Poems: Second Series, verges perilously on the riddle. And it often happens that her passionate devotion to concise statement in terms of metaphor left for her readers a small rich emblem of which the colors tease, the thought entices, but the meaning escapes. Against this, however, should be set her capacity when occasion came, for a granite simplicity, any parallel to which one must seek in the seventeenth century. This, for example, called "Parting."

> My life closed twice before its close;
> It yet remains to see
> If Immortality unveil
> A third event to me,
>
> So huge, so hopeless to conceive,
> As these that twice befell.
> Parting is all we know of heaven
> And all we need of hell.

Or this, from Poems: First Series:

> I died for beauty, but was scarce
> Adjusted in the tomb,
> When one who died for truth was lain
> In an adjoining room.
>
> He questioned softly why I failed?
> 'For beauty,' I replied.
> 'And I for truth,—the two are one;
> We brethren are,' he said.
>
> And so, as kinsmen met at night,
> We talked between the rooms,
> Until the moss had reached our lips,
> And covered up our names.

Both these poems, it will be noted, deal with death; and it must be observed that the number of poems by Miss Dickinson on this subject is one of the most remarkable things about her. Death, and the problem of life after death, obsessed her. She seems to have thought of it constantly—she died all her life, she probed death daily. "That bareheaded life under grass worries one like a wasp," she wrote. Ultimately, the obsession became morbid, and her eagerness for details, after the death of a friend—the hungry desire to know *how* she died—became almost vulture-like. But the preoccupation, with its horrible uncertainties—its doubts about immortality, its hatred of the flesh, and its many reversals of both positions—gave us her sharpest work. The theme was inexhaustible for her. If her poetry seldom became "lyrical," seldom departed from the colorless sobriety of its bare iambics and toneless assonance, it did so most of all when the subject was death. Death profoundly and cruelly invited her. It was most of all when she tried "to touch the smile," and dipped her "fingers in the frost," that she took full possession of her genius.

Her genius was, it remains to say, as erratic as it was brilliant. Her disregard for accepted forms or for regularities was incorrigible. Grammar, rhyme, meter—anything went by the board if it stood in the way of thought or freedom of utterance. Sometimes this arrogance was justified; sometimes not. She did not care in the least for variety of effect—of her six hundred-odd poems practically all are in octosyllabic quatrains or couplets, sometimes with rhyme, sometimes with assonance, sometimes with neither. Everywhere, when one first comes to these poems, one seems to see nothing but a colorless dry monotony. How deceptive a monotony, concealing what reserves of depth and splendor; what subtleties of mood and tone! Once adjust oneself to the spinsterly angularity of the mode, its lack of eloquence or rhetorical speed, its naïve and often prosaic directness, one discovers felicities of thought and phrase on every page. The magic is terse and sure. And ultimately one simply sighs at Miss Dickinson's singular perversity, her lapses and tyrannies, and accepts them as an inevitable part of the strange and original genius she was. The lapses and tyrannies become a positive charm—one even suspects they were deliberate. They satisfied her—therefore they satisfy us. This marks, of course, our complete surrender to her highly individual gift, and to the singular sharp beauty, present everywhere, of her personality. The two things cannot be separated; and together, one must suppose, they suffice to put her among the finest poets in the language.

Emily Dickinson

by *Allen Tate*

Great poetry needs no special features of difficulty to make it mysterious. When it has them, the reputation of the poet is likely to remain
uncertain. This is still true of Donne, and it is true of Emily Dickinson,
whose verse appeared in an age unfavorable to the use of intelligence in
poetry. Her poetry is not like any other poetry of her time; it is not like
any of the innumerable kinds of verse written today. In still another
respect it is far removed from us. It is a poetry of ideas, and it demands
of the reader a point of view—not an opinion of the New Deal or of
the League of Nations, but an ingrained philosophy that is fundamental,
a settled attitude that is almost extinct in this eclectic age. Yet it is not
the sort of poetry of ideas which, like Pope's, requires a point of view
only. It requires also, for the deepest understanding, which must go
beneath the verbal excitement of the style, a highly developed sense of
the specific quality of poetry—a quality that most persons accept as the
accidental feature of something else that the poet thinks he has to say.
This is one reason why Miss Dickinson's poetry has not been widely read.

There is another reason, and it is a part of the problem peculiar to
a poetry that comes out of fundamental ideas. We lack a tradition of
criticism. There were no points of critical reference passed on to us from
a preceding generation. I am not upholding here the so-called dead hand
of tradition, but rather a rational insight into the meaning of the present
in terms of some imaginable past implicit in our own lives: we need
a body of ideas that can bear upon the course of the spirit and yet remain coherent as a rational instrument. We ignore the present, which
is momently translated into the past, and derive our standards from
imaginative constructions of the future. The hard contingency of fact
invariably breaks these standards down, leaving us the intellectual chaos
which is the sore distress of American criticism. Marxian criticism has
become the lastest disguise of this heresy.

Still another difficulty stands between us and Miss Dickinson. It is the failure of the scholars to feel more than biographical curiosity about her. We have scholarship, but that is no substitute for a critical tradition. Miss Dickinson's value to the research scholar, who likes historical difficulty for its own sake, is slight; she is too near to possess the remoteness of literature. Perhaps her appropriate setting would be the age of Cowley or of Donne. Yet in her own historical setting she is, nevertheless, remarkable and special.

Although the intellectual climate into which she was born, in 1830, had, as all times have, the features of a transition, the period was also a major crisis culminating in the war between the States. After that war, in New England as well as in the South, spiritual crises were definitely minor until the First World War.

Yet, a generation before the war of 1861-65, the transformation of New England had begun. When Samuel Slater in 1790 thwarted the British embargo on mill machinery by committing to memory the whole design of a cotton spinner and bringing it to Massachusetts, he planted the seed of the "Western spirit." By 1825 its growth in the East was rank enough to begin choking out the ideas and habits of living that New England along with Virginia had kept in unconscious allegiance to Europe. To the casual observer, perhaps, the New England character of 1830 was largely an eighteenth-century character. But theocracy was on the decline, and industrialism was rising—as Emerson, in an unusually lucid moment, put it, "Things are in the saddle." The energy that had built the meeting-house ran the factory.

Now the idea that moved the theocratic state is the most interesting historically of all American ideas. It was, of course, powerful in seventeenth-century England, but in America, where the long arm of Laud could not reach, it acquired an unchecked social and political influence. The important thing to remember about the puritan theocracy is that it permeated, as it could never have done in England, a whole society. It gave final, definite meaning to life, the life of pious and impious, of learned and vulgar alike. It gave—and this is its significance for Emily Dickinson, and in only slightly lesser degree for Melville and Hawthorne —it gave an heroic proportion and a tragic mode to the experience of the individual. The history of the New England theocracy, from Apostle Eliot to Cotton Mather, is rich in gigantic intellects that broke down— or so it must appear to an outsider—in a kind of moral decadence and depravity. Socially we may not like the New England idea. Yet it had an immense, incalculable value for literature: it dramatized the human soul.

But by 1850 the great fortunes had been made (in the rum, slave, and milling industries), and New England became a museum. The whatnots groaned under the load of knickknacks, the fine china dogs and cats, the pieces of Oriental jade, the chips off the leaning tower of Pisa. There were the rare books and the cosmopolitan learning. It was all equally displayed as the evidence of a superior culture. The Gilded Age had already begun. But culture, in the true sense, was disappearing. Where the old order, formidable as it was, had held all this personal experience, this eclectic excitement, in a comprehensible whole, the new order tended to flatten it out in a common experience that was not quite in common; it exalted more and more the personal and the unique in the interior sense. Where the old-fashioned puritans got together on a rigid doctrine, and could thus be individualists in manners, the nineteenth-century New Englander, lacking a genuine religious center, began to be a social conformist. The common idea of the Redemption, for example, was replaced by the conformist idea of respectability among neighbors whose spiritual disorder, not very evident at the surface, was becoming acute. A great idea was breaking up, and society was moving toward external uniformity, which is usually the measure of the spiritual sterility inside.

At this juncture Emerson came upon the scene: the Lucifer of Concord, he had better be called hereafter, for he was the light-bearer who could see nothing but light, and was fearfully blind. He looked around and saw the uniformity of life, and called it the routine of tradition, the tyranny of the theological idea. The death of Priam put an end to the hope of Troy, but it was a slight feat of arms for the doughty Pyrrhus; Priam was an old gentleman and almost dead. So was theocracy; and Emerson killed it. In this way he accelerated a tendency that he disliked. It was a great intellectual mistake. By it Emerson unwittingly became the prophet of a piratical industrialism, a consequence of his own transcendental individualism that he could not foresee. He was hoist with his own petard.

He discredited more than any other man the puritan drama of the soul. The age that followed, from 1865 on, expired in a genteel secularism, a mildly didactic order of feeling whose ornaments were Lowell, Longfellow, and Holmes. "After Emerson had done his work," says Mr. Robert Penn Warren, "any tragic possibilities in that culture were dissipated." Hawthorne alone in his time kept pure, in the primitive terms, the primitive vision; he brings the puritan tragedy to its climax. Man, measured by a great idea outside himself, is found wanting. But for Emerson man is greater than any idea and, being himself the Over-Soul, is innately perfect; there is no struggle because—I state the Emersonian doctrine, which is very slippery, in its extreme terms—because there is no possibility of error. There is no drama in human character because there is no tragic fault. It is not surprising, then, that after Emerson New England literature tastes like a sip of cambric tea. Its center of vision has disappeared. There is Hawthorne looking back, there is Emerson looking not too clearly at anything ahead: Emily Dickinson, who has in her something of both, comes in somewhere between.

With the exception of Poe there is no other American poet whose work so steadily emerges, under pressure of certain disintegrating obsessions, from the framework of moral character. There is none of whom it is truer to say that the poet *is* the poetry. Perhaps this explains the zeal of her admirers for her biography; it explains, in part at least, the gratuitous mystery that Mrs. Bianchi, a niece of the poet and her official biographer, has made of her life. The devoted controversy that Miss Josephine Pollitt and Miss Genevieve Taggard started a few years ago with their excellent books shows the extent to which the critics feel the intimate connection of her life and work. Admiration and affection are pleased to linger over the tokens of a great life; but the solution to the Dickinson enigma is peculiarly superior to fact.

The meaning of the identity—which we merely feel—of character and poetry would be exceedingly obscure, even if we could draw up a kind of Binet correlation between the two sets of "facts." Miss Dickinson was a recluse; but her poetry is rich with a profound and varied experience. Where did she get it? Now some of the biographers, nervous in the presence of this discrepancy, are eager to find her a love affair, and I think this search is due to a modern prejudice: we believe that no virgin can know enough to write poetry. We shall never learn where she got the rich quality of her mind. The moral image that we have of Miss Dickinson stands out in every poem; it is that of a dominating spinster whose very sweetness must have been formidable. Yet her poetry constantly moves within an absolute order of truths that overwhelmed her simply because to her they were unalterably fixed. It is dangerous to assume that her "life," which to the biographers means the thwarted love affair she is supposed to have had, gave to her poetry a decisive direction. It is even more dangerous to suppose that it made her a poet.

Poets are mysterious, but a poet, when all is said, is not much more mysterious than a banker. The critics remain spellbound by the technical license of her verse and by the puzzle of her personal life. Personality is a legitimate interest because it is an incurable interest, but legitimate as a personal interest only; it will never give up the key to anyone's verse. Used to that end, the interest is false. "It is apparent," writes Mr. Conrad Aiken, "that Miss Dickinson became a hermit by deliberate and conscious choice"—a sensible remark that we cannot repeat too often. If it were necessary to explain her seclusion with disappointment in love, there would remain the discrepancy between what the seclusion produced and the seclusion looked at as a cause. The effect, which is her poetry, would imply the whole complex of anterior fact, which was the social and religious structure of New England.

The problem to be kept in mind is thus the meaning of her "deliberate and conscious" decision to withdraw from life to her upstairs room. This simple fact is not very important. But that it must have been her sole way of acting out her part in the history of her culture, which made, with the variations of circumstance, a single demand upon all its representatives —this is of the greatest consequence. All pity for Miss Dickinson's "starved life" is misdirected. Her life was one of the richest and deepest ever lived on this continent.

When she went upstairs and closed the door, she mastered life by rejecting it. Others in their way had done it before; still others did it later. If we suppose—which is to suppose the improbable—that the love affair precipitated the seclusion, it was only a pretext; she would have found another. Mastery of the world by rejecting the world was the doctrine, even if it was not always the practice, of Jonathan Edwards and Cotton Mather. It is the meaning of fate in Hawthorne: his people are fated to withdraw from the world and to be destroyed. And it is one of the great themes of Henry James.

There is a moral emphasis that connects Hawthorne, James, and Miss Dickinson, and I think it is instructive. Between Hawthorne and James lies an epoch. The temptation to sin, in Hawthorne, is, in James, transformed into the temptation not to do the "decent thing." A whole world-scheme, a complete cosmic background, has shrunk to the dimensions of the individual conscience. This epoch between Hawthorne and James lies in Emerson. James found himself in the post-Emersonian world, and he could not, without violating the detachment proper to an artist, undo Emerson's work; he had that kind of intelligence which refuses to break its head against history. There was left to him only the value, the historic role, of rejection. He could merely escape from the physical presence of that world which, for convenience, we may call Emerson's world: he could only take his Americans to Europe upon the vain quest of something that they had lost at home. His characters, fleeing the wreckage of the puritan culture, preserved only their honor. Honor became a sort of forlorn hope struggling against the forces of "pure fact" that had got loose in the middle of the century. Honor alone is a poor weapon against nature, being too personal, finical, and proud, and James achieved a victory by refusing to engage the whole force of the enemy.

In Emily Dickinson the conflict takes place on a vaster field. The enemy to all those New Englanders was Nature, and Miss Dickinson saw into the character of this enemy more deeply than any of the others. The general symbol of Nature, for her, is Death, and her weapon against Death is the entire powerful dumb-show of the puritan theology led by Redemption and Immortality. Morally speaking, the problem for James and Miss Dickinson is similar. But her advantages were greater than his. The advantages lay in the availability to her of the puritan ideas on the theological plane.

These ideas, in her poetry, are momently assailed by the disintegrating force of Nature (appearing as Death) which, while constantly breaking them down, constantly redefines and strengthens them. The values are purified by the triumphant withdrawal from Nature, by their power to recover from Nature. The poet attains to a mastery over experience by facing its utmost implications. There is the clash of powerful opposites, and in all great poetry—for Emily Dickinson is a great poet—it issues in a tension between abstraction and sensation in which the two elements may be, of course, distinguished logically, but not really. We are shown our roots in Nature by examining our differences with Nature; we are renewed by Nature without being delivered into her hands. When it is possible for a poet to do this for us with the greatest imaginative comprehension, a possibility that the poet cannot himself create, we have the perfect literary situation. Only a few times in the history of English poetry has this situation come about: notably, the period between about 1580 and the Restoration. There was a similar age in New England from which emerged two talents of the first order—Hawthorne and Emily Dickinson.

There is an epoch between James and Miss Dickinson. But between her and Hawthorne there exists a difference of intellectual quality. She lacks almost radically the power to seize upon and understand abstractions for their own sake; she does not separate them from the sensuous illuminations that she is so marvelously adept at; like Donne, she *perceives abstraction* and *thinks sensation*. But Hawthorne was a master of ideas, within a limited range; this narrowness confined him to his own kind of life, his own society, and out of it grew his typical forms of experience, his steady, almost obsessed vision of man; it explains his depth and intensity. Yet he is always conscious of the abstract, doctrinal aspect of his mind, and when his vision of action and emotion is weak, his work becomes didactic. Now Miss Dickinson's poetry often runs into quasi-homiletic forms, but it is never didactic. Her very ignorance, her lack of formal intellectual training, preserved her from the risk that imperiled Hawthorne. She cannot reason at all. She can only *see*. It is impossible to imagine what she might have done with drama or fiction; for, not approaching the puritan temper and through it the puritan myth, through human action, she is able to grasp the terms of the myth directly and by a feat that amounts almost to anthropomorphism, to give them a luminous tension, a kind of drama, among themselves.

One of the perfect poems in English is "The Chariot," and it illustrates better than anything else she wrote the special quality of her mind. I think it will illuminate the tendency of this discussion:

> Because I could not stop for death,
> He kindly stopped for me;
> The carriage held but just ourselves
> And immortality.
>
> We slowly drove, he knew no haste,
> And I had put away
> My labor, and my leisure too,
> For his civility.

We passed the school where children played,
Their lessons scarcely done;
We passed the fields of gazing grain,
We passed the setting sun.

We paused before a house that seemed
A swelling of the ground;
The roof was scarcely visible,
The cornice but a mound.

Since then 'tis centuries; but each
Feels shorter than the day
I first surmised the horses' heads
Were toward eternity.

If the word "great" means anything in poetry, this poem is one of the greatest in the English language. The rhythm charges with movement the pattern of suspended action back of the poem. Every image is precise and, moreover, not merely beautiful, but fused with the central idea. Every image extends and intensifies every other. The third stanza especially shows Miss Dickinson's power to fuse, into a single order of perception, a heterogeneous series: the children, the grain, and the setting sun (time) have the same degree of credibility; the first subtly preparing for the last. The sharp *gazing* before *grain* instills into nature a cold vitality of which the qualitative richness has infinite depth. The content of death in the poem eludes explicit definition. He is a gentleman taking a lady out for a drive. But note the restraint that keeps the poet from carrying this so far that it becomes ludicrous and incredible; and note the subtly inter-fused erotic motive, which the idea of death has presented to most roman-tic poets, love being a symbol interchangeable with death. The terror of death is objectified through this figure of the genteel driver, who is made ironically to serve the end of Immortality. This is the heart of the poem: she has presented a typical Christian theme in its final irresolution, with-out making any final statements about it. There is no solution to the prob-lem; there can be only a presentation of it in the full context of intellect and feeling. A construction of the human will, elaborated with all the abstracting powers of the mind, is put to the concrete test of experience: the idea of immortality is confronted with the fact of physical disintegra-tion. We are not told what to think; we are told to look at the situation.

The framework of the poem is, in fact, the two abstractions, mortality and eternity, which are made to associate in equality with the images: she sees the ideas, and thinks the perceptions. She did, of course, nothing of the sort; but we must use the logical distinctions, even to the extent of paradox, if we are to form any notion of this rare quality of mind. She could not in the proper sense think at all, and unless we prefer the feeble poetry of moral ideas that flourished in New England in the eighties, we must conclude that her intellectual deficiency contributed at least negatively to her great distinction. Miss Dickinson is probably the only Anglo-American poet of her century whose work exhibits the perfect literary situation—in which is possible the fusion of sensibility and thought. Unlike her contemporaries, she never succumbed to her ideas, to easy solutions, to her private desires.

Philosophers must deal with ideas, but the trouble with most nineteenth-century poets is too much philosophy; they are nearer to being philosophers than poets, without being in the true sense either. Tennyson is a good example of this; so is Arnold in his weak moments. There have been poets like Milton and Donne, who were not spoiled for their true business by leaning on a rational system of ideas, who understood the poetic use of ideas. Tennyson tried to mix a little Huxley and a little Broad Church, without understanding either Broad Church or Huxley; the result was fatal, and what is worse, it was shallow. Miss Dickinson's ideas were deeply imbedded in her character, not taken from the latest tract. A conscious cultivation of ideas in poetry is always dangerous, and even Milton escaped ruin only by having an instinct for what in the deepest sense he understood. Even at that there is a remote quality in Milton's approach to his material, in his treatment of it; in the nineteenth century, in an imperfect literary situation where literature was confused with documentation, he might have been a pseudo-philosopher-poet. It is difficult to conceive Emily Dickinson and John Donne succumbing to rumination about "problems"; they would not have written at all.

Neither the feeling nor the style of Miss Dickinson belongs to the seventeenth century; yet between her and Donne there are remarkable ties. Their religious ideas, their abstractions, are momently toppling from the rational plane to the level of perception. The ideas, in fact, are no longer the impersonal religious symbols created anew in the heat of emotion, that we find in poets like Herbert and Vaughan. They have become, for Donne, the terms of personality; they are mingled with the miscellany of sensation. In Miss Dickinson, as in Donne, we may detect a singularly morbid concern, not for religious truth, but for personal revelation. The modern word is self-exploitation. It is egoism grown irresponsible in religion and decadent in morals. In religion it is blasphemy; in society it means usually that culture is not self-contained and sufficient, that the spiritual community is breaking up. This is, along with some other features that do not concern us here, the perfect literary situation.

II

Personal revelation of the kind that Donne and Miss Dickinson strove for, in the effort to understand their relation to the world, is a feature of all great poetry; it is probably the hidden motive for writing. It is the effort of the individual to live apart from a cultural tradition that no longer sustains him. But this culture, which I now wish to discuss a little, is indispensable: there is a great deal of shallow nonsense in modern criticism which holds that poetry—and this is a half-truth that is worse than false—is essentially revolutionary. It is only indirectly revolutionary: the intellectual and religious background of an age no longer contains the whole spirit, and the poet proceeds to examine that background in terms of immediate experience. But the background is necessary; otherwise all the arts (not only poetry) would have to rise in a vacuum. Poetry does not dispense with tradition; it probes the deficiencies of a tradition. But it must have a tradition to probe. It is too bad that Arnold did not explain his doctrine, that poetry is a criticism of life, from the viewpoint of its background: we should have been spared an era of academic misconception, in which criticism of life meant a diluted pragmatism, the criterion of which was respectability. The poet in the true sense "criticizes" his tradition, either as such, or indirectly by comparng it with something that is about to replace it; he does what the root-meaning of the verb implies—he *discerns* its real elements and thus establishes its value, by putting it to the test of experience.

What is the nature of a poet's culture? Or, to put the question properly, what is the meaning of culture for poetry? All the great poets become the material of what we popularly call culture; we study them to acquire it. It is clear that Addison was more cultivated than Shakespeare; nevertheless Shakespeare is a finer source of culture than Addison. What is the meaning of this? Plainly it is that learning has never had anything to do with culture except instrumentally: the poet must be exactly literate enough to write down fully and precisely what he has to say, but no more. The source of a poet's true culture lies back of the paraphernalia of culture, and not all the historical activity of an enlightened age can create it.

A culture cannot be consciously created. It is an available source of ideas that are imbedded in a complete and homogeneous society. The poet finds himself balanced upon the moment when such a world is about to fall, when it threatens to run out into looser and less self-sufficient impulses. This world order is assimilated, in Miss Dickinson, as medievalism was in Shakespeare, to the poetic vision; it is brought down from abstraction to personal sensibility.

In this connection it may be said that the prior conditions for great poetry, given a great talent, may be reduced to two: the thoroughness of the poet's discipline in an objective system of truth, and his lack of consciousness of such a discipline. For this discipline is a number of fundamental ideas the origin of which the poet does not know; they give form and stability to his fresh perceptions of the world; and he cannot shake them off. This is his culture, and, like Tennyson's God, it is nearer than hands and feet. With reasonable certainty we unearth the elements of

Shakespeare's culture, and yet it is equally certain—so innocent was he of his own resources—that he would not know what our discussion is about. He appeared at the collapse of the medieval system as a rigid pattern of life, but that pattern remained in Shakespeare what Shelley called a "fixed point of reference" for his sensibility. Miss Dickinson, as we have seen, was born into the equilibrium of an old and a new order. Puritanism could not be to her what it had been to the generation of Cotton Mather—a body of absolute truths; it was an unconscious discipline timed to the pulse of her life.

The perfect literary situation: it produces, because it is rare, a special and perhaps the most distinguished kind of poet. I am not trying to invent a new critical category. Such poets are never very much alike on the surface; they show us all the varieties of poetic feeling; and, like other poets, they resist all classification but that of temporary convenience. But, I believe, Miss Dickinson and John Donne would have this in common: their sense of the natural world is not blunted by a too-rigid system of ideas; yet the ideas, the abstractions, their education or their intellectual heritage, are not so weak as to let their immersion in nature, or their purely personal quality, get out of control. The two poles of the mind are not separately visible; we infer them from the lucid tension that may be most readily illustrated by polar activity. There is no thought as such at all; nor is there feeling; there is that unique focus of experience which is at once neither and both.

Like Miss Dickinson, Shakespeare is without opinions; his peculiar merit is also deeply involved in his failure to think about anything; his meaning is not in the content of his expression; it is in the tension of the dramatic relations of his characters. This kind of poetry is at the opposite of intellectualism. (Miss Dickinson is obscure and difficult, but that is not intellectualism.) To T. W. Higginson, the editor of *The Atlantic Monthly,* who tried to advise her, she wrote that she had no education. In any sense that Higginson could understand, it was quite true. His kind of education was the conscious cultivation of abstractions. She did not reason about the world she saw; she merely saw it. The "ideas" implicit in the world within her rose up, concentrated in her immediate perception.

That kind of world at present has for us something of the fascination of a buried city. There is none like it. When such worlds exist, when such cultures flourish, they support not only the poet but all members of society. For, from these, the poet differs only in his gift for exhibiting the structure, the internal lineaments, of his culture by threatening to tear them apart: a process that concentrates the symbolic emotions of society while it seems to attack them. The poet may hate his age; he may be an outcast like Villon; but this world is always there as the background to what he has to say. It is the lens through which he brings nature to focus and control—the clarifying medium that concentrates his personal feeling.

It is ready-made; he cannot make it; with it, his poetry has a spontaneity and a certainty of direction that, without it, it would lack. No poet could have invented the ideas of "The Chariot"; only a great poet could have found their imaginative equivalents. Miss Dickinson was a deep mind writing from a deep culture, and when she came to poetry, she came infallibly.

Infallibly, at her best; for no poet has ever been perfect, nor is Emily Dickinson. Her precision of statement is due to the directness with which the abstract framework of her thought acts upon its unorganized material. The two elements of her style, considered as point of view, are immortality, or the idea of permanence, and the physical process of death or decay. Her diction has two corresponding features: words of Latin or Greek origin and, sharply opposed to these, the concrete Saxon element. It is this verbal conflict that gives her verse its high tension; it is not a device deliberately seized upon, but a feeling for language that senses out the two fundamental components of English and their metaphysical relation: the Latin for ideas and the Saxon for perceptions—the peculiar virtue of English as a poetic language.

Like most poets Miss Dickinson often writes out of habit; the style that emerged from some deep exploration of an idea is carried on as verbal habit when she has nothing to say. She indulges herself:

> There's something quieter than sleep
> Within this inner room!
> It wears a sprig upon its breast,
> And will not tell its name.
>
> Some touch it and some kiss it,
> Some chafe its idle hand;
> It has a simple gravity
> I do not understand!
>
> While simple hearted neighbors
> Chat of the "early dead,"
> We, prone to periphrasis,
> Remark that birds have fled!

It is only a pert remark; at best a superior kind of punning—one of the worst specimens of her occasional interest in herself. But she never had the slightest interest in the public. Were four poems or five published in her lifetime? She never felt the temptation to round off a poem for public exhibition. Higginson's kindly offer to make her verse "correct" was an invitation to throw her work into the public ring—the ring of Lowell and Longfellow. He could not see that he was tampering with one of the rarest literary integrities of all time. Here was a poet who had no use for the supports of authorship—flattery and fame; she never needed money.

She had all the elements of a culture that has broken up, a culture that on the religious side takes its place in the museum of spiritual antiquities. Puritanism, as a unified version of the world, is dead; only a remnant of it in trade may be said to survive. In the history of puritanism she comes between Hawthorne and Emerson. She has Hawthorne's matter, which a too irresponsible personality tends to dilute into a form like Emerson's; she is often betrayed by words. But she is not the poet of personal sentiment; she has more to say than she can put down in any one poem. Like Hardy and Whitman, she must be read entire; like Shakespeare, she never gives up her meaning in a single line.

She is therefore a perfect subject for the kind of criticism which is chiefly concerned with general ideas. She exhibits one of the permanent relations between personality and objective truth, and she deserves the special attention of our time, which lacks that kind of truth.

She has Hawthorne's intellectual toughness, a hard, definite sense of the physical world. The highest flights to God, the most extravagant metaphors of the strange and the remote, come back to a point of casuistry, to a moral dilemma of the experienced world. There is, in spite of the homiletic vein of utterance, no abstract speculation, nor is there a message to society; she speaks wholly to the individual experience. She offers to the unimaginative no riot of vicarious sensation; she has no useful maxims for men of action. Up to this point her resemblance to Emerson is slight: poetry is a sufficient form of utterance, and her devotion to it is pure. But in Emily Dickinson the puritan world is no longer self-contained; it is no longer complete; her sensibility exceeds its dimensions. She has trimmed down its supernatural proportions; it has become a morality; instead of the tragedy of the spirit there is a commentary upon it. Her poetry is a magnificent personal confession, blasphemous and, in its self-revelation, its honesty, almost obscene. It comes out of an intellectual life toward which it feels no moral responsibility. Cotton Mather would have burnt her for a witch.

Emily Dickinson and the Limits of Judgment

by Yvor Winters

Antiquest felt at noon
When August, burning low,
Calls forth this spectral canticle,
Repose to typify.

When the poems of Emily Dickinson first began to appear, in the years shortly following her death, she enjoyed a period of notoriety and of semi-popularity that endured for perhaps ten years; after about ten years of semi-obscurity, her reputation was revived with the publication of *The Single Hound,* and has lasted unabated to the present day, though with occasional signs that it may soon commence to diminish. A good many critics have resented her reputation, and it has not been hard for them to justify their resentment; probably no poet of comparable reputation has been guilty of so much unpardonable writing. On the other hand, one cannot shake off the uncomfortable feeling that her popularity has been mainly due to her vices; her worst poems are certainly her most commonly praised, and as a general matter, great lyric poetry is not widely read or admired.

The problem of judging her better poems is much of the time a subtle one. Her meter, at its worst—that is, most of the time—is a kind of stiff sing-song; her diction, at its worst, is a kind of poetic nursery jargon; and there is a remarkable continuity of manner, of a kind nearly indescribable, between her worst and her best poems. The following poem will illustrate the defects in perfection:

I like to see it lap the miles,
And lick the valleys up,
And stop to feed itself at tanks;
And then, prodigious, step

> Around a pile of mountains,
> And, supercilious, peer
> In shanties by the sides of roads;
> And then a quarry pare
>
> To fit its sides, and crawl between,
> Complaining all the while
> In horrid, hooting stanza;
> Then chase itself down hill
>
> And neigh like Boanerges;
> Then, punctual as a star,
> Stop—docile and omnipotent—
> At its own stable door.

The poem is abominable; and the quality of silly playfulness which renders it abominable is diffused more or less perceptibly throughout most of her work, and this diffusion is facilitated by the limited range of her metrical schemes.

The difficulty is this: that even in her most nearly perfect poems, even in those poems in which the defects do not intrude momentarily in a crudely obvious form, one is likely to feel a fine trace of her countrified eccentricity; there is nearly always a margin of ambiguity in our final estimate of even her most extraordinary work, and though the margin may appear to diminish or disappear in a given reading of a favorite poem, one feels no certainty that it will not reappear more obviously with the next reading. Her best poems, quite unlike the best poems of Ben Jonson, of George Herbert, or of Thomas Hardy, can never be isolated certainly and defensibly from her defects; yet she is a poetic genius of the highest order, and this ambiguity in one's feeling about her is profoundly disturbing. The following poem is a fairly obvious illustration; we shall later see less obvious:

> I started early, took my dog,
> And visited the sea;
> The mermaids in the basement
> Came out to look at me,
>
> And frigates in the upper floor
> Extended hempen hands,
> Presuming me to be a mouse
> Aground, upon the sands.
>
> But no man moved me till the tide
> Went past my simple shoe,
> And past my apron and my belt,
> And past my bodice too,

And made as he would eat me up
As wholly as a dew
Upon a dandelion's sleeve—
And then I started too.

And he—he followed close behind;
I felt his silver heel
Upon my ankle,—then my shoes
Would overflow with pearl.

Until we met the solid town,
No man he seemed to know;
And bowing with a mighty look
At me, the sea withdrew.

The mannerisms are nearly as marked as in the first poem, but whereas the first poem was purely descriptive, this poem is allegorical and contains beneath the more or less mannered surface an ominously serious theme, so that the manner appears in a new light and is somewhat altered in effect. The sea is here the traditional symbol of death; that is, of all the forces and qualities in nature and in human nature which tend toward the dissolution of human character and consciousness. The playful protagonist, the simple village maiden, though she speaks again in the first person, is dramatized, as if seen from without, and her playfulness is somewhat restrained and formalized. Does this formalization, this dramatization, combined with a major symbolism, suffice effectually to transmute in this poem the quality discerned in the first poem, or does that quality linger as a fine defect? The poem is a poem of power; it may even be a great poem; but this is not to answer the question. I have never been able to answer the question.

Her poetic subject matter might be subdivided roughly as follows: natural description; the definition of moral experience, including the definition of difficulties of comprehension; and mystical experience, or the definition of the experience of "immortality," to use a favorite word, or of beatitude. The second subdivision includes a great deal, and her best work falls within it; I shall consider it last. Her descriptive poems contain here and there brilliant strokes, but she had the hard and uncompromising approach to experience of the early New England Calvinists; lacking all subtlety, she displays the heavy hand of one unaccustomed to fragile objects; her efforts at lightness are distressing. Occasionally, instead of endeavoring to treat the small subject in terms appropriate to it, she endeavors to treat it in terms appropriate to her own temperament, and we have what appears a deliberate excursion into obscurity, the subject being inadequate to the rhetoric, as in the last stanza of the poem beginning, "At half-past three a single bird":

> At half-past seven, element
> Nor implement was seen,
> And place was where the presence was,
> Circumference between.

The stanza probably means, roughly, that bird and song alike have disappeared, but the word "circumference," a resonant and impressive one, is pure nonsense.

This unpredictable boldness in plunging into obscurity, a boldness in part, perhaps, inherited from the earlier New Englanders whose sense of divine guidance was so highly developed, whose humility of spirit was commonly so small; a boldness dramatized by Melville in the character of Ahab; this congenital boldness may have led her to attempt the rendering of purely theoretic experience, the experience of life after death. There are numerous poems which attempt to express the experience of posthumous beatitude, as if she were already familiar with it; the poetic terms of the expression are terms, either abstract or concrete, of human life, but suddenly fixed, or approaching fixation, as if at the cessation of time in eternity, as if to the dead the living world appeared as immobile as the dead person appears to the living, and the fixation frequently involves an element of horror:

> Great streets of silence led away
> To neighborhoods of pause;
> Here was no notice, no dissent,
> No universe, no laws.

> By clocks 'twas morning, and for night
> The bells at distance called;
> But epoch had no basis here,
> For period exhaled.

The device here employed is to select a number of terms representing familiar abstractions or perceptions, some of a commonplace nature, some relatively grandiose or metaphysical, and one by one to negate these terms; a number of statements, from a grammatical point of view, have been made, yet actually no concrete image emerges, and the idea of the poem—the idea of the absolute dissidence of the eternal from the temporal—is stated indirectly, and, in spite of the brevity of the poem and the gnomic manner, with extraordinary redundancy. We come painfully close in this poem to the irresponsible playfulness of the poem about the railway train; we have gone beyond the irresponsible obscurity of the poem about the bird.

This is technically a mystical poem: that is, it endeavors to render an experience—the rapt contemplation, eternal and immovable, which Aquinas describes as the condition of beatitude—which is by definition foreign to all human experience, yet to render it in terms of a modified human experience. Yet there is no particular reason to believe that Emily Dickinson was a mystic, or thought she was a mystic. The poems of this variety, and there are many of them, appear rather to be efforts to dramatize an idea of salvation, intensely felt, but as an idea, not as something experienced, and as an idea essentially inexpressible. She deliberately utilizes imagery irrelevant to the state with which she is concerned, because she cannot do otherwise; yet the attitude toward the material, the attitude of rapt contemplation, is the attitude which she presumably expects to achieve toward something that she has never experienced. The poems are invariably forced and somewhat theoretical; they are briskly clever, and lack the obscure but impassioned conviction of the mystical poems of Very; they lack the tragic finality, the haunting sense of human isolation in a foreign universe, to be found in her greatest poems, of which the explicit theme is a denial of this mystical trance, is a statement of the limits of judgment.

There are a few curious and remarkable poems representing a mixed theme, of which the following is perhaps the finest example:

> Because I could not stop for Death,
> He kindly stopped for me;
> The carriage held but just ourselves
> And Immortality.
>
> We slowly drove, he knew no haste,
> And I had put away
> My labor, and my leisure too,
> For his civility.
>
> We passed the school where children played
> At wrestling in a ring;
> We passed the fields of gazing grain,
> We passed the setting sun.
>
> We paused before a house that seemed
> A swelling of the ground;
> The roof was scarcely visible,
> The cornice but a mound.
>
> Since then 'tis centuries; but each
> Feels shorter than the day
> I first surmised the horse's heads
> Were toward eternity.

In the fourth line we find the familiar device of using a major abstraction in a somewhat loose and indefinable manner; in the last stanza there is the semi-playful pretence of familiarity with the posthumous experience of eternity, so that the poem ends unconvincingly though gracefully, with a formulary gesture very roughly comparable to that of the concluding couplet of many an Elizabethan sonnet of love; for the rest the poem is a remarkably beautiful poem on the subject of the daily realization of the imminence of death—it is a poem of departure from life, an intensely conscious leave-taking. In so far as it concentrates on the life that is being left behind, it is wholly successful; in so far as it attempts to experience the death to come, it is fraudulent, however exquisitely, and in this it falls below her finest achievement. Allen Tate, who appears to be unconcerned with this fraudulent element, praises the poem in the highest terms; he appears almost to praise it for its defects[1]: "The sharp *gazing* before *grain* instills into nature a kind of cold vitality of which the qualitative richness has infinite depth. The content of death in the poem eludes forever any explicit definition . . . she has presented a typical Christian theme in all its final irresolution, without making any final statement about it." The poem ends in irresolution in the sense that it ends in a statement that is not offered seriously; to praise the poem for this is unsound criticism, however. It is possible to solve any problem of insoluble experience by retreating a step and defining the boundary at which comprehension ceases, and by then making the necessary moral adjustments to that boundary; this in itself is an experience both final and serious, and it is the experience on which our author's finest work is based.

Let me illustrate by citation. The following poem defines the subject which the mystical poems endeavor to conceal: the soul is taken to the brink of the incomprehensible, and is left there, for retreat is impossible, and advance is impossible without a transmutation of the soul's very nature. The third and fourth lines display the playful redundancy of her weaker poems, but the intrusion of the quality here is the result of habit, and is a minor defect; there is nothing in the conception of the poem demanding a compromise. There is great power in the phrasing of the remainder of the poem, especially in the middle stanza:

> Our journey had advanced;
> Our feet were almost come
> To that odd fork in Being's road,
> Eternity by term.

> Our pace took sudden awe,
> Our feet reluctant led.
> Before were cities, but between
> The forest of the dead.

[1] Allen Tate, *Reactionary Essays on Poetry and Ideas* (New York: Charles Scribner's Sons, 1936). The essay on Emily Dickinson. [See previous essay by Tate in this volume.]

> Retreat was out of hope,—
> Behind, a sealèd route,
> Eternity's white flag before,
> And God at every gate.

She is constantly defining the absolute cleavage between the living and the dead. In the following poem the definition is made more powerfully, and in other terms:

> 'Twas warm at first, like us,
> Until there crept thereon
> A chill, like frost upon a glass,
> Till all the scene be gone.
>
> The forehead copied stone,
> The fingers grew too cold
> To ache, and like a skater's brook
> The busy eyes congealed.
>
> It straightened—that was all—
> It crowded cold to cold—
> It multiplied indifference
> As Pride were all it could.
>
> And even when with cords
> 'Twas lowered like a freight,
> It made no signal, nor demurred,
> But dropped like adamant.

The stiffness of phrasing, as in the barbarously constructed fourth and twelfth lines, is allied to her habitual carelessness, yet in this poem there is at least no triviality, and the imagery of the third stanza in particular has tremendous power.

The poem beginning, "The last night that she lived," treats the same theme in more personal terms; the observer watches the death of a friend, that is follows the friend to the brink of the comprehensible, sees her pass the brink, and faces the loss. The poem contains a badly mixed figure and at least two major grammatical blunders, in addition to a little awkward inversion of an indefensible variety, yet there is in the poem an immediate seizing of terrible fact, which makes it, at least fragmentarily, very great poetry:

> And we, we placed the hair,
> And drew the head erect;
> And then an awful leisure was,
> Our faith to regulate.

Her inability to take Christian mysticism seriously did not, however, drive her to the opposite extreme of the pantheistic mysticism which was seducing her contemporaries. The following lines, though not remarkable poetry, are a clear statement of a position consistently held:

> But nature is a stranger yet;
>   The ones that cite her most
> Have never passed her haunted house,
>   Nor simplified her ghost.
>
> To pity those that know her not
>   Is helped by the regret
> That those who know her, know her less
>   The nearer her they get.

Nature as a symbol, as Allen Tate has pointed out in the essay to which I have already referred, remains immitigably the symbol of all the elements which corrupt, dissolve, and destroy human character and consciousness; to approach nature is to depart from the fullness of human life, and to join nature is to leave human life. Nature may thus be a symbol of death, representing much the same idea as the corpse in the poem beginning " 'Twas warm at first, like us," but involving a more complex range of association.

In the following poem, we are shown the essential cleavage between man, as represented by the author-reader, and nature, as represented by the insects in the late summer grass; the subject is the plight of man, the willing and freely-moving entity, in a universe in which he is by virtue of his essential qualities a foreigner. The intense nostalgia of the poem is the nostalgia of man for the mode of being which he perceives imperfectly and in which he cannot share. The change described in the last two lines is the change in the appearance of nature and in the feeling of the observer which results from a recognition of the cleavage:

> Farther in summer than the birds,
> Pathetic from the grass,
> A minor nation celebrates
> Its unobtrusive mass.
>
> No ordinance is seen,
> So gradual the grace,
> A pensive custom it becomes,
> Enlarging loneliness.
>
> Antiquest felt at noon
> When August, burning low,
> Calls forth this spectral canticle,
> Repose to typify.

> Remit as yet no grace,
> No furrow on the glow,
> Yet a druidic difference
> Enhances nature now.

The first two lines of the last stanza are written in the author's personal grammatical short hand; they are no doubt defective in this respect, but the defect is minor. They mean: There is as yet no diminution of beauty, no mark of change on the brightness. The twelfth line employs a meaningless inversion. On the other hand, the false rhymes are employed with unusually fine modulation; the first rhyme is perfect, the second and third represent successive stages of departure, and the last a return to what is roughly the stage of the second. These effects are complicated by the rhyming, both perfect and imperfect, from stanza to stanza. The intense strangeness of this poem could not have been achieved with standard rhyming. The poem, though not quite one of her most nearly perfect, is probably one of her five or six greatest, and is one of the most deeply moving and most unforgettable poems in my own experience; I have the feeling of having lived in its immediate presence for many years.

The three poems which combine her greatest power with her finest execution are strangely on much the same theme, both as regards the idea embodied and as regards the allegorical embodiment. They deal with the inexplicable fact of change, of the absolute cleavage between successive states of being, and it is not unnatural that in two of the poems this theme should be related to the theme of death. In each poem, seasonal change is employed as the concrete symbol of the moral change. This is not the same thing as the so-called pathetic fallacy of the romantics, the imposition of a personal emotion upon a physical object incapable either of feeling such an emotion or of motivating it in a human being. It is rather a legitimate and traditional form of allegory, in which the relationships between the items described resemble exactly the relationships between certain moral ideas or experiences; the identity of relationship evoking simultaneously and identifying with each other the feelings attendant upon both series as they appear separately. Here are the three poems, in the order of the seasons employed, and in the order of increasing complexity both of theme and of technique:

1

> A light exists in spring
> Not present in the year
> At any other period.
> When March is scarcely here

A color stands abroad
On solitary hills
That science cannot overtake,
But human nature feels.

It waits upon the lawn;
It shows the furthest tree
Upon the furthest slope we know;
It almost speaks to me.

Then, as horizons step,
Or noons report away,
Without the formula of sound,
It passes, and we stay:

A quality of loss
Affecting our content,
As trade had suddenly encroached
Upon a sacrament.

2

As imperceptibly as grief
The Summer lapsed away,—
Too imperceptible, at last,
To seem like perfidy.

A quietness distilled,
As twilight long begun,
Or Nature, spending with herself
Sequestered afternoon.

The dusk drew earlier in,
The morning foreign shone,—
A courteous, yet harrowing grace,
As guest who would be gone.

And thus, without a wing,
Or service of a keel,
Our summer made her light escape
Into the beautiful.

3

There's a certain slant of light,
On winter afternoons,
That oppresses, like the weight
Of cathedral tunes.

Heavenly hurt it gives us;
We can find no scar,
But internal difference
Where the meanings are.

None may teach it anything,
'Tis the seal, despair,—
An imperial affliction
Sent us of the air.

When it comes, the landscape listens,
Shadows hold their breath;
When it goes, 'tis like the distance
On the look of death.

In the seventh, eighth, and twelfth lines of the first poem, and, it is barely possible, in the seventh and eighth of the third, there is a very slight echo of the brisk facility of her poorer work; the last line of the second poem, perhaps, verges ever so slightly on an easy prettiness of diction, though scarcely of substance. These defects are shadowy, however; had the poems been written by another writer, it is possible that we should not observe them. On the other hand, the directness, dignity, and power with which these major subjects are met, the quality of the phrasing, at once clairvoyant and absolute, raise the poems to the highest level of English lyric poetry.

The meter of these poems is worth careful scrutiny. The basis of all three is the so-called Poulter's Measure, first employed, if I remember aright, by Surrey, and after the time of Sidney in disrepute. It is the measure, however, not only of the great elegy on Sidney commonly attributed to Fulke Greville, but of some of the best poetry between Surrey and Sidney, including the fine poem by Vaux on contentment and the great poem by Gascoigne in praise of a gentlewoman of dark complexion. The English poets commonly though not invariably wrote the poem in two long lines instead of four short ones, and the lines so conceived were the basis of their rhetoric. In the first of the three poems just quoted, the measure is employed without alteration, but the short line is the basis of the rhetoric; an arrangement which permits of more varied adjustment of sentence to line than if the long line were the basis. In the second poem, the first stanza is composed not in the basic measure, but in lines of eight, six, eight, and six syllables; the shift into the normal six, six, eight, and six in the second stanza, as in the second stanza of the poem beginning, "Farther in summer," results in a subtle and beautiful muting both of meter and of tone. This shift she employs elsewhere, but especially in poems of four stanzas, to which it appears to have a natural relationship; it is a brilliant technical invention.

In the third poem she varies her simple base with the ingenuity and mastery of a virtuoso. In the first stanza, the two long lines are reduced to seven syllables each, by the dropping of the initial unaccented syllable; the second short line is reduced to five syllables in the same manner. In the second stanza, the first line, which ought now to be of six syllables, has but five metrical syllables, unless we violate normal usage and count the second and infinitely light syllable of *Heaven*, with an extrametrical syllable at the end, the syllable dropped being again the initial one; the second line, which ought to have six syllables, has likewise lost its initial syllable, but the extrametrical *us* of the preceding line, being unaccented, is in rhythmical effect the first syllable of the second line, so that this syllable serves a double and ambiguous function—it maintains the syllable-count of the first line, in spite of an altered rhythm, and it maintains the rhythm of the second line in spite of the altered syllable-count. The third and fourth lines of the second stanza are shortened to seven and five. In the third stanza the first and second lines are constructed like the third and fourth of the second stanza; the third and fourth lines like the first and second of the second stanza, except that in the third line the initial unaccented syllable is retained; that is, the third stanza repeats the construction of the second, but in reverse order. The final stanza is a triumphant resolution of the three preceding: the first and third lines, like the second and fourth, are metrically identical; the first and third contain seven syllables each, with an additional extrametrical syllable at the end which takes the place of the missing syllable at the beginning of each subsequent short line, at the same time that the extrametrical syllable functions in the line in which it is written as part of a two-syllable rhyme. The elaborate structure of this poem results in the balanced hesitations and rapid resolutions which one hears in reading it. This is metrical artistry at about as high a level as one is likely to find it.

Emily Dickinson was a product of the New England tradition of moral Calvinism; her dissatisfaction with her tradition led to her questioning most of its theology and discarding much of it, and led to her reinterpreting some of it, one would gather, in the direction of a more nearly Catholic Christianity. Her acceptance of Christian moral concepts was unimpaired, and the moral tone of her character remained immitigably Calvinistic in its hard and direct simplicity. As a result of this Calvinistic temper, she lacked the lightness and grace which might have enabled her to master minor themes; she sometimes stepped without hesitation into obscurantism, both verbal and metaphysical. But also as a result of it, her best poetry represents a moral adjustment to certain major moral problems which are carefully defined; it is curious in the light of this fact, and in the light of the publicization which they have received, that her love poems never equal her highest achievement—her best work is on themes more generalized and inclusive.

Emily Dickinson differed from every other major New England writer of the nineteenth century, and from every major American writer of the century save Melville, of those affected by New England, in this: that her New England heritage, though it made her life a moral drama, did not leave her life in moral confusion. It impoverished her in one respect, however: of all great poets, she is the most lacking in taste; there are innumerable beautiful lines and passages wasted in the desert of her crudities; her defects, more than those of any other great poet that I have read, are constantly at the brink, or pushing beyond the brink, of her best poems. This stylistic character is the natural product of the New England which produced the barren little meeting houses; of the New England founded by the harsh and intrepid pioneers, who in order to attain salvation trampled brutally through a world which they were too proud and too impatient to understand. In this respect, she differs from Melville, whose taste was rich and cultivated. But except by Melville, she is surpassed by no writer that this country has produced; she is one of the greatest lyric poets of all time.

American Humor

by George F. Whicher

. . . The habit of combining small and great was ingrained in Emily Dickinson to such an extent that she instinctively employed it again and again in her most serious poems. When, reversing the humorous device of using the grand to express the trivial, she projected a tremendous meaning into a homely image, she not infrequently laid herself open to the suspicion of making light of sacred things or of sporting with tender feelings. But in all probability she had no thought of being flippant. A way of speaking that might afford amusement if applied to light or indifferent subjects remained her constant manner even when she dealt with her most piercing memories and profound reflections. She was able to separate any circumstance or idea at will from the sentiment normally attached to it, and thus make available for artistic use what otherwise would shock or dazzle the mind into inarticulateness.

This power of detachment, this sense of doubleness, originally fostered by the Puritan genius for introspection, was confirmed by her early saturation in humor of the frontier type. "We make a thing humorous," says Professor Cazamian, "by expressing it with a certain twist, a queer reserve, an inappropriateness, and as it were an unconsciousness of what we all the time feel it to be." This is a perfect description of the quality that Emily acquired and practiced. For the joke's sake she learned to resist the impulses of sentiment as completely as Mark Twain himself. The professional imperviousness to normal feeling evident in some of his journalistic sketches, as for example in "Cannibalism in the Cars," and in the jocular treatment of horror in general may be paralleled by bits of ruthless comedy scattered through her letters:

> Who writes those funny accidents, where railroads meet each other unexpectedly, and gentlemen in factories get their heads cut off quite informally? The author, too, relates them in such a sprightly way, that they are quite attractive. Vinnie was disappointed to-night, that there were not more accidents—I read the news aloud while Vinnie was sewing.

Add to this parlor bloodthirstiness a sample of mortuary merriment:

> No one has called so far, but one old lady to look at a house. I directed
> her to the cemetery to spare expense of moving.

This is a side of the sensitive and tenderly sympathetic Emily that is often
overlooked. In many of her serious poems we may note a similar aloofness
from the emotion implied, an odd quirk of incongruous association that
in a less poignant connection we should unhesitatingly recognize as wit.
It was Emily Dickinson's special faculty to stand undismayed in the midst
of convulsions, some unshaken particle in her consciousness ready to note
with ironical detachment the reeling of the brain.

Examples are not far to seek. If she encountered a painful disillusion-
ment, she was as apt as not to picture it as the shattering of a dish "on
the stones at bottom of my mind" (54, cxviii). The momentousness of
death to her imagination did not prevent her from stating the anguish of
bereavement in terms of broom and dustpan (166, xxii):

> The sweeping up the heart,
> And putting love away
> We shall not want to use again
> Until eternity.

In a letter of 1860-61 to her Norcross cousins Emily echoed mischievously the routine question of the clerk behind the counter, "Is there
nothing else?" Not long afterward, perhaps, this trite phrase blended in
unexpected coalescence with her insistent cry, "Is God love's adversary?"
Her frustration merged with glee as she contrived to exhibit an indifferent
Providence in the figure of a village storekeeper:

> The mighty merchant smiled.
>
> Brazil? He twirled a button,
> Without a glance my way:
> "But, madam, is there nothing else
> That we can show to-day?"

And, finally, her genuine reverence could not repress her delight when
she detected an apt metaphor for "God so loved the world that he sent his
only begotten Son" in *The Courtship of Miles Standish:*

> God is a distant, stately Lover,
> Woos, so He tells us, by His Son.
> Surely a vicarious courtship!
> Miles' and Priscilla's such a one.

To prevent any such outcome as that in Longfellow's poem, God the Divine Lover vouches that—in terms of the metaphor—Miles Standish and John Alden are one and the same; a move of "hyperbolic archness" on God's part.

We need not agree with an incensed clerical reader of the 1890's who characterized this last outburst as "one of the most offensive pieces of Unitarianism ever published." Emily was not mocking the Trinity when she ran out the parallel; she was too absorbed in her mind's adventure to regard the niceties of pious sentiment. What was originally a faculty of humorous expression was transformed in these poems and many others into a highly individual and effective poetic idiom. To grasp the soul at white heat she needed more than ever the tongs that wit supplied. Complete integrity in what lay too deep for tears was possible only by indirection. And more profoundly, the detachment implied in a whimsical turn of mind was auxiliary to the complete independence of stereotyped sentiments that alone makes possible the writing of distinguished lyric poetry.

> If nothing larger than a World's
> Departure from a hinge,
> Or Sun's extinction be observed,
> 'Twas not so large that I
> Could lift my forehead from my work
> For curiosity.

Emily felt both the arrogant self-concentration of a lyric poet and the instinct for comedy that is deeply implanted in the American nature. The latter is woven into the fabric of her poems and cannot easily be separated for analysis. It startles us in an unexpected phrase or epithet and is gone before we know it, as though a bird in flight had slightly lowered an eyelid at us. A few of her poems, however, are controlled throughout by comic intention. One of the signs is an abrupt change of key, as in "Lightly stepped a yellow star" (242, lviii), where for six lines Emily revels in a luxuriance of rippling *l*'s accompanied by the moonlight suggestiveness of such words as *silver* and *lustral*. When the poem reaches its utmost effect of artful loveliness, she drops unexpectedly into a conversational tone that lets us down with a bump. The final *l*-sound of *punctual*, echoing in a totally different context all the preceding *l*'s, knits the poem together in a "musical joke."

> All of evening softly lit
> As an astral hall—
> "Father," I observed to Heaven,
> "You are punctual."

Think for a moment of the well-known passage in *A Tramp Abroad* where Mark Twain describes an enchanting young girl at the opera, lavishing on her a rhapsody of adjectives, only to puncture the shimmering bubble of loveliness by letting her exclaim: "Auntie, I just *know* I've got five hundred fleas on me!" That in coarse terra cotta is the counterpart of what Emily wrought in porcelain. The design, abstractly considered, is the same. . . .

Romantic Sensibility

by Henry W. Wells

The contrasted seeds of mysticism and Stoicism took root in Emily's mind not only because of her own personality, but through a congenial ground prepared for them by romantic sensibility. From a remote past ultimately came the two of her most precious heritages. But from her own cultural age she prudently drew what it had best to give. In view of her total accomplishments she is neither a mystic nor a stoic poet, though she undeniably is both mystical and stoical. Neither can her total achievement be labelled or confined by such descriptive epithets as classical, romantic, or modern. In some degree answering to each specification, her total stature can best be described in the phrase shrewdly noted by her biographer: "this was a poet." Nevertheless for a rounded appreciation of her art, recognition of its definitely romantic quality is essential, since no major aspect of her work can be properly grasped while others are disregarded. Her mind was integrated at least to the extent that such qualities as her peculiar mysticism and Stoicism are themselves properly explained only in the light of her romantic environment and soul.

Just as it is true that Emily remains far from wholly romantic, so it is clear that the whole of Romanticism in the historical sense is not to be traced in her own work. Singularly free from many of the qualities of her contemporaries or immediate predecessors, she has little specifically in common with the romantic poets, either of her own time of Tennyson, Browning, Swinburne, and Arnold, or the earlier period of Wordsworth, Coleridge, Keats, and Shelley. That she revolted from a Calvinistic training which she could never wholly forget, by no means makes her a follower of Byron, whose thought thus far, at least, followed hers. That she devoured Scott's tales, in no way allied her creative mind to the acknowledged master of the early nineteenth-century novel. She well knew that she followed her own star. Yet the popularity of her poems when first published, far surpassing the expectations of her editors and publishers, proves her to have been in some respects indigenous to her age. The woman who confessed that, whether with or against her will, she perforce saw "New Englandly," must have known that she also saw to some extent in the light of her age, coincident with the height of the Romantic Movement. Her conscious aims to retain the fresh imagination of childhood, to celebrate the self, to praise nature, and to indulge freely in fancy, stood among the most conspicuous ideals in the literature of her century. Although in the last analysis both her spirit and her style break violently with leading cultural patterns of the century, she was still its child, however naughty and rebellious. In no respect did she comply more closely than in cultivating the richest and most conspicuous vein in romantic thought as a whole, namely the new sensibility.

This sensibility is a mental state both in life and art accentuating the emotional life. Under circumstances which would at any time evoke strong feelings, romantic theory and practice made them still stronger; under conditions which would hardly be expected to elicit emotional responses at all, this sensibility begot an ample flow of sentiment. To the romantics, feeling became a badge of distinction, just as in the Restoration world "wit" was so regarded. Artifice became social practice, or, in Oscar Wilde's words, life imitated art. The familiar story requires no retelling here, but should be at least recalled. Women kneaded their emotions into a refined state of sensitivity, while men affected effeminacy. Soft phrases and melting airs grew to be marks of polite society. It was ingeniously contrived to man's temporary comfort and lasting discomfort that as industrial society grew uglier the personal life grew more refined. This hyper-development of purely personal reactions accompanied the rise of revolutionary individualism and *laissez faire* at the same time that it soothed the old or more conservative regimes into a forgetfulness of social ills known only too well. Radicals and conservatives differed on almost all scores save one, but in that one respect happily concurred. Virtually all men and women loved the poem or novel of sentiment. Sensibility was the cultural slogan of the age. The man of feeling became the man of distinction. Whereas Aristotle, arch-master of the classically minded, advocated the stern elimination of pity and fear, romantic leaders in poetry and fiction founded their art upon a shameless exploitation of these very emotions. Sympathy and terror ruled the imagination of the Revolutionary Age, and even governed much of its practice. Sympathizing with the conditions of the poor, revolutionaries aimed to relieve their poverty and reduce the hard inequalities of opportunity. Conservatives found social utility in focussing in private life the emotionalism indulged by the reformers in their attitudes toward society. Both dwelt with fond sorrow over their own misfortunes. Art and literature evolved into a vast hyperbole of passion; effeminacy, or at best a literature more appropriate to the feminine boudoir than the masculine forum, gained ascendency; sentimental clichés distorted style; in time it grew even more fashionable to pity one's self than to pity the poor; and, finally, with so many forced, affected, and abnormal attitudes disfiguring a fundamentally morbid society, neurotic elements tyrannized in art and poetry, and very nearly dominated all fields of aesthetic expression. Shelley's career perfectly represents the usual course traversed by the romantic author, and —what is more important—epitomizes the evolution of the entire movement. He began by pitying the poor and ended by pitying himself.

All these too-well-known qualities, for better and for worse, inevitably leave some marks on Emily's verse. Though never sentimental to the degree of hypocrisy, nor extravagant to that of vulgarity, she utilizes her age for the best interests of her art, and occasionally commits the inevitable mistakes. In no other period, perhaps, could her writing have acquired such warmth; in none could it have fallen victim to the peculiar lapses which at times prevent it from attaining greatness.

Certain passages are the most conspicuous in betokening her romantic background. A number of her poems offer particularly apt illustration of the romantic tendency to indulge an hyperbole of emotionalism. "Dare you see a soul at the white heat?" is, for example, a lyric admirably in key with its first line. There is a touch of self-consciousness here, not as yet precisely a weakness, but indicative of the true romantic spirit. Certain of Emily's verses show a keen awareness of the physical states of the body induced by extremes of nervous excitement. They are paralleled by her account of true poetry itself, which, as told to the incredulous Colonel Higginson, she identified as an experience making her "feel physically as though the top of my head were taken off." Her verse abounds in trembling, freezing, and burning. The following is indicative:

> It was not frost, for on my flesh
> I felt siroccos crawl,—
> Nor fire, for just my marble feet
> Could keep a chancel cool.

The verse of this tightly restrained New Englander contains many images drawn from volcanic fires. Significantly enough, volcanoes fascinated and haunted her. Their "reticent" ways, periodically giving place to violent irruption, paralleled her own experiences and the behavior of her friends and family.

> A crater I may contemplate,
> Vesuvius at home.

One commentator has somewhat boldly equated this Vesuvius with the outbreaks of her father's anger. Although some of her most moving love poems are majestically impersonal, or, in other words, come nearer to Sappho or Dante than to Browning or Tennyson, a number by no means of her least impressive pieces are stamped with marks of peculiarly romantic sensibility. One of her best known lyrics, "Although I put away his life," is very much in Mrs. Browning's equally sentimental and realistic manner. Emily dreams of a connubial happiness that has failed to be realized. She might have been the faithful and devoted servant of a husband, sowing the flowers he preferred, soothing his pains, pushing pebbles from his path, playing his favorite tunes, or fetching him his slippers. The more fanciful of her love hyperboles also tend to follow current patterns. One of her longest lyrics, "I cannot live with you," proves a more concise version of the romantic theme of love and immortality as handled in Rossetti's *Blessed Damosel*. Emily vividly describes her own sensitivity in language unmistakably romantic, as when she asks the rhetorical question why a bird at daybreak

> Should stab my ravished spirit
> With dirks of melody.

She is even critical of her own romantic excesses. In finely romantic diction she voices the fear that her lines may drip overmuch and have too red a glow:

> Sang from the heart, Sire,
> Dipped my beak in it.
> If the tune drip too much,
> Have a tint too red,
>
> Pardon the cochineal,
> Suffer the vermilion,
> Death is the wealth
> Of the poorest bird,

Without losing high merit, Emily's verse occasionally steps down from a high and impersonal dignity to assume the consciously feminine manner especially admired in the mid-nineteenth century. Though the poetry is more than commonplace it is less than universal. The feminine note grows unmistakable. This is heard most clearly in the poem describing a girl's excitement on receiving a message from her lover: "The way I read a letter's thus." In a manner which Samuel Richardson would have approved, she tells how she locks the door, fingers the envelope, glances nervously about to assure herself of absolute privacy, and, finally, reads the words of a lover whose identity she coyly declines to disclose. "I am ashamed, I hide," describes in some detail a bride's bashfulness according to the most familiar romantic ideals. "Wert thou but ill," similarly describes the bride who romantically protests that she will follow her lover through a series of the most trying misfortunes. Much of the sentiment in Emily's nature poetry also betrays the age of sensibility. This shows clearly in a little poem, "To lose, if one can find again." The poet tenderly covers over her garden, hopefully awaiting springtime resurrection, as she confidently expects reunion in heaven with her beloved.

Even though Emily never descends to the baser moods of self-pity, it would be superficial to overlook the romantic poignance which her verses occasionally attain through a tendency in this perilous direction. "I was the slightest in the house," she writes, in an autobiographical poem somewhat exaggerating her own social limitations. With similar self-consciousness she addresses herself as, "the favorite of doom." "Don't put up my thread and needle," she writes, in a tender and genuine piece descriptive of her own hopes and fears in time of dangerous sickness. In several of her poems, as the notable, " 'Twas just this time last year I died," she indulges the melancholy fancy that she is dead, and wonders how gravely or how lightly the family will cherish her memory. Such poetry affords a nice contrast to the same theme treated in the witty and cynical Augustan manner in Swift's remarkable lines, *On the Death of Dean Swift*.

After the unabashed fashion of romantic poets, Emily at times unhesitatingly exposes the more neurotic features of her personality. Such writing falls into the emphatically self-conscious romantic idiom. With powerful imagery she describes the gingerly walk of the neurotic genius through the terrifying jungles of experience: "I stepped from plank to plank." She discloses the painful tensions within the pathological soul. In one poem, "The body grows outside," she describes the soul as hiding behind the flesh. In another, "Me from Myself to banish," she reveals the agonies of the split personality, pains of which she must herself have been poignantly aware. Briefly, at least, she probes the tragic abyss of her own sub-conscious: "The subterranean freight, The cellars of the soul." In a tragic poem, "Had we our senses," she suggests that men would become even madder if they saw clearly into their own madness. Sanity is merely the integument of an invincible stupidity. Baudelaire himself could have proposed no more cynical a view.

These various romantic attitudes Emily shares and explores, without as a rule falling victim to the typical banalities of her times, either in meaning or expression. In other words, her poetry shares the deeper and grander qualities of her chief contemporaries without sinking for any length of time into the commonplaces of romantic thought, sentiment, and style. In this regard it becomes appropriate to note a few instances in which her language or her images come close to losing the sharpness and distinction of her own literary personality. "Glee! the great storm is over!" for instance, approximates the style of the typical, undistinguished romantic ballad. The rhymes are commonplace: "land—sand"; "souls—shoals"; "door—more"; "eye—reply". The meter is painfully regular. The symbols of sailors shipwrecked or saved hardly achieve distinction. Longfellow himself might have written the final line: "And only the waves reply." The poem has a saving irony which is Emily's own and preserves it from bathos; but it remains extremely romantic.

Another lyric, "Good night! which put the candle out?" is comprised of a series of all-too-familiar romantic images drawn from home or the sea. In still another, "Forever cherished be the tree," the image of two robins as two angels has the customary nineteenth-century extravagance with little assurance of Emily's better genius. In short, to her contacts with the Romantic Age she owed a small but very definite part of her artistic success; and much the greater part of her by no means fatal faults. Her devotion to "eternity" may have been due in part to a distrust, at times latent and at times highly conscious, of the dominating fashions of her times. Although she distrusted Romanticism, she was too shrewd to discard it altogether.

The Communication of the Word

by Donald E. Thackrey

"In the beginning was the word." Emily Dickinson probably would have accepted a literal interpretation of this opening phrase of the Gospel of St. John. Language and comunication exercised an almost hypnotic fascination over her; the power of the individual word, in particular, seems to have inspired her with nothing less than reverence. Such an attitude toward words is an important aspect of Emily Dickinson's approach to poetry in that it partially accounts for her method of composition and helps explain her use of poetic composition to discipline the mystical intuitions which involved her in both ecstasy and suffering of extreme intensity. This chapter is devoted to discovering the essential viewpoints of Emily Dickinson in regard to the power for communication of the individual word.

It seems certain that Emily Dickinson approached the writing of poetry inductively—that is, through the combining of words to arrive at whatever conclusion the word pattern seemed to suggest, rather than using words as subordinate instruments in expressing a total conception. Her amazing inconsistency of intellectual position may have resulted in part from the practice of starting with individual words and manipulating them into brilliant patterns regardless of the direction of thought, instead of always orienting her poems within an integrated philosophy. One notices how many of her poems seem less concerned with a total conception than with expressing a series of staccato inspirations occurring to her in the form of individual words. The following poem is remarkable in its use of words; its meaning, however, is somewhat obscured by the constant impact of words which seem to be separate entities refusing to assume a subordinate position in the poem.

> A nearness to Tremendousness
> An Agony procures,
> Affliction ranges Boundlessness.

"The Communication of the Word." From *Emily Dickinson's Approach to Poetry* (Lincoln: University of Nebraska Press, 1954) by Donald E. Thackrey. (University of Nebraska Studies, New Series No. 13.) Reprinted by permission of the University of Nebraska Press.

Vicinity to laws
Contentment's quiet suburb,—
Affliction cannot stay
In acre or location—
It rents Immensity.[1]

The poem contrasts contentment with affliction. One is orderly, secluded, innocuous; the other is unrestrained, passionate, infinite. However, the excessive weight of such words as *Tremendousness, Boundlessness, Immensity* together with the extraordinary implications of the words *procures, ranges, suburb, rents,* all overflowing one small stanza is more than a reader can grasp without dividing the poem into its elements and studying each word individually.

Emily Dickinson herself gives us ample warrant for studying her poems a word at a time. Her constant practice of compiling a thesaurus of word choices for a single line, while constituting grave editorial difficulty, is at least an indication that each word was a veritable dynamo of implication and associations. Mrs. Bingham gives an interesting account in *Ancestors' Brocades* of the abundant presence of alternative words in the Dickinson manuscripts. She cites an example occurring in the poem "The Bible is an antique volume" of which the final lines read in manuscript:

Had but the tale a thrilling, typic,
  hearty, bonnie, breathless, spacious,
  tropic, warbling, ardent, friendly,
  magic, pungent, winning, mellow
  teller
All the boys would come—
Orpheus's sermon captivated,
It did not condemn.[2]

Each of the variant adjectives apparently occurred to her as refined gradations or aspects of her total conception. Her consequent reluctance to choose a single word now poses the almost insuperable editorial problem of determining which word she probably would have preferred. In the instance above, *warbling* was selected out of the possible fourteen choices. Many of the published poems themselves exhibit a similar concern with individual words. Note the accumulation of verbs in the following stanza.

[1] *Poems*, p. 453, No. cxxx. [Martha Dickinson Bianchi and Alfred Leete Hampson, eds., *The Poems of Emily Dickinson* (Boston: Little, Brown & Co., 1937).]
[2] Millicent Todd Bingham, *Ancestors' Brocades: The Literary Debut of Emily Dickinson* (New York: Harper & Row, Publishers, 1945), p. 37.

'Tis this invites, appals, endows,
Flits, glimmers, proves, dissolves,
Returns, suggests, convicts, enchants—
Then flings in Paradise! [3]

Emily Dickinson wrote one poem specifically about the choice of words.

"Shall I take thee?" the poet said
To the propounded word.
"Be stationed with the candidates
Till I have further tried."

The poet probed philology
And when about to ring
For the suspended candidate,
There came unsummoned in

That portion of the vision
The word applied to fill.
Not unto nomination
The cherubim reveal. [4]

This poem is extremely instructive in indicating Emily Dickinson's actual method of composition and in suggesting the relationship between rational labor and inspiration. The two instances of the numerous word "candidates" partly fulfill the poet's intention but also suggest new words which more aptly represent further aspects of the total conception. Soon the train of "candidates" has exhausted every facet and implication of the idea, and in doing so has securely established the fully developed idea in the poet's mind. But still no one word is adequate to the idea. As, the poet attempts to choose the best alternative, the "cherubim" of artistic inspiration reveal the precise word which completes the "vision." It is significant that the revealed word comes "unsummoned" in a flash of intuition. Such a word admits of no hesitation or doubt in the poet's mind. And yet the implication of the poem is that the revealing of the word must be preceded by the preparatory, conscious, rational effort of probing philology. Perhaps we can assume that the long series of "nominations" with no indicated choice which occur in some of her manuscript poems represent occasions when a portion of the vision was not filled by the revelation of the cherubim. She herself was well aware that inspiration, while all-sufficient when present, seldom came even to a great poet.

[3] *Poems*, p. 352, No. cxxxii.
[4] *Bolts of Melody*, p. 228, No. 436.

Your thoughts don't have words every day,
They come a single time
Like signal esotoric sips
Of sacramental wine,

Which while you taste so native seems,
So bounteous, so free,
You cannot comprehend its worth
Nor its infrequency.[5]

Even in friendly letters Emily Dickinson apparently could never escape the significance and implication of the words she used. In a letter in which she wrote the sentence, "Thank you for remembering me," there is the reflection immediately following it, "Remembrance—mighty word." [6] So conscious of particular words was she that the use of an especially significant word in a letter stimulated a parenthetical exclamation written perhaps with the desire to share with her friend something of her own intoxication with words.

The most evident characteristic of words, as far as Emily Dickinson was concerned, is their startling vitality. Her poems indicate that she regarded words as organic—separate little entities with a being, growth, and immortality of their own.

A word is dead
When it is said,
Some say.
I say it just
Begins to live
That day.[7]

The life of the spoken word does not depend upon the duration of sound vibrations but is an inextricable part of the experience and being of the speaker and those to whom he speaks. Thus a word, no matter how simple, may be charged with imperishable significance because of its intimate relationship with human minds and souls. Connotations and symbolic extensions of meaning become inseparable from the word, so that its pronouncement will forever stimulate an entire "circumference" of meaning in addition to its denotative definition. In the following poem the idea of the immortality of words which are expressions of and inevitable associations with significant experience is clearly stated.

[5] *Ibid.,* p. 228, No. 435.
[6] *Letters,* p. 248. [Mabel Loomis Todd, *The Letters of Emily Dickinson* (Cleveland: The World Publishing Co., 1951).]
[7] *Poems,* p. 42, No. lxxxix.

A little overflowing word
That any hearing had inferred
For ardor or for tears,
Though generations pass away,
Traditions ripen and decay,
As eloquent appears.[8]

Eloquence, of course, did not mean for Emily Dickinson longwinded-ness, or unusual figures of speech, or any formal consideration; it meant the effective thrust of meaning stripped of everything that might qualify, ornament, or weaken it. Much of her imagery chosen to describe the effect of a word upon him who hears it supports the contention that, for her, communication consisted in transmitting or perceiving an immediate, overpowering vision.

There is a word
Which bears a sword
Can pierce an armed man.
It hurls its barbed syllables,—
At once is mute again.[9]

Communication is a *sword*. It *pierces*. *Barbed* syllables are *hurled*. There is no room here for slow comprehension, perception aided by illustration and analogy, and understanding based on a cautious consideration and analysis of a statement. There is only the overpowering immediacy of the piercing word. The sword imagery is elaborated in the following stanza.

She dealt her pretty words like blades,
As glittering they shone,
And every one unbared a nerve
Or wantoned with a bone.[10]

Emily Dickinson testified that the concept of the "sword eloquence" of words was not a theoretical speculation for her, but was a personal, vivid reality. Consider, for example, how the sound of her lover's name affected her.

I got so I could hear his name
Without—

[8] *Ibid.*, p. 269, No. cxxxvi.
[9] *Ibid.*, p. 148, No. xliv.
[10] *Ibid.*, p. 290, No. xxix.

> Tremendous gain!—
> That stop-sensation in my soul,
> And thunder in the room.[11]

Eloquence, however, even in the sharpened sense in which she used the term, was not the real nature of words for Emily Dickinson. The eloquence was only the flash of light a calm ocean surface reflects. Deeper than light penetrates there is the turbulence of an unseen tide. Words seemed to her to embody some terrifying, mysterious power which approached omnipotence. She knew that such power was not suspected by most people who ordinarily used words glibly and thoughtlessly. And she apparently believed that even she herself could only sense the existence of this power and never fully perceive its extent.

> Could any mortal lip divine
>   The undeveloped freight
> Of a delivered syllable,
>   'Twould crumble with the weight.[12]

The power of words, while a great source of wonder and delight for her, was not regarded as wholly beneficial. No great power is entirely hazardless. "What a hazard an accent is! When I think of the hearts it has scuttled or sunk, I almost fear to lift my hand to so much as a punctuation." [13] And in one poem she even compares words with malignant germs.

> A word dropped careless on a page
> May stimulate an eye,
> When folded in perpetual seam
> The wrinkled author lie.
>
> Infection in the sentence breeds;
> We may inhale despair
> At distances of centuries
> From the malaria.[14]

Emily Dickinson seems fascinated with the thought that words once expressed assume an existence of their own and can never be recalled by their "wrinkled author." In a letter she warns, "We must be careful

[11] *Ibid.*, p. 370, No. clxvi.
[12] *Ibid.*, p. 45, No. xcv.
[13] *Letters*, p. 364.
[14] Millicent Todd Bingham, "Poems of Emily Dickinson: Hitherto Published Only in Part," *New England Quarterly*, XX (March, 1947), 15.

what we say. No bird resumes its egg." [15] She then copies the first stanza
of the poem just quoted, replacing the word *stimulate* with the word
consecrate and the word *dropped* with the word *left*. The meaning of
the stanza is now different but the fundamental expression of the potency
and endurance of "a word" remains unchanged.

An interesting aspect of Emily Dickinson's reverence for words is the
way in which she frequently uses terms of language and communication
to describe or symbolize something entirely different from communication in the ordinary sense of the term. For instance in a poem beginning,
"Step lightly on this narrow spot!" she says that a certain dead person's
name is told as far as "fame export / Her deathless syllable." [16] In another
poem the concept of love is symbolized by the phrases of endearment
between lovers which eclipse all other communication.

> Many a phrase has the English language,—
> I have heard but one
>
> .   .   .   .
>
> Breaking in bright orthography
> On my simple sleep;
>
> .   .   .   .
>
> Say it again—Saxon!
> Hush—only to me! [17]

Even natural objects were described in terms implying human communication.

> The hills in purple syllables
> The day's adventures tell
> To little groups of continents
> Just going home from school.[18]

Occasionally she uses language terms in writing about death. The mystery
of death has often been called a "riddle" by poets, but Emily Dickinson
endows that word with unusual power by making it a separate, vital
entity—a technique characteristic of her emphasis upon the individual
word. One poem begins, "I have not told my garden yet," and the last
stanza reads:

> Nor lisp it at the table,
> Nor heedless by the way

[15] *Letters,* p. 233.
[16] *Poems,* p. 176, No. xliv.
[17] *Ibid.,* p. 422, No. lxxvii.
[18] *Bolts of Melody,* p. 92, No. 166.

Hint that within the riddle
One will walk to-day! [19]

The "riddle" becomes an existing locality or condition—something into
which one can walk. After stepping within the riddle, Emily Dickinson
suggests, one is still helpless without the power and the grace of the
Divine. Such power is inevitably described in terms of language.

The quiet nonchalance of death
No daybreak can bestir;
The slow archangel's syllables
Must awaken her. [20]

And in "Tis whiter than an Indian pipe," Emily Dickinson describes the
awakened spirit as a "limitless hyperbole." [21] In the same type of metaphor she pictures herself as a syllable in the poem beginning, "I could
suffice for Him."

"Would I be whole?" He sudden broached.
My syllable rebelled . . .[22]

Her answer, or more generally, her powers of communication are identified with herself.

It seems likely that Emily Dickinson would have devoted herself to
individual words if only because she keenly realized their vital power
in both of its aspects—the sudden lightning flash, and the deep, undeveloped freight. Apparently she delighted in words for their own sake,
as most of us do only as children. She admittedly was childlike in many
respects and indeed consciously sought to maintain in herself the eagerness and wonder of a child. Thus it is not inconsistent with her attitude
and general approach to experience that she should savor the sounds
and meanings of words just as a child experiments and practices with
his first syllables.

However, Emily Dickinson had a more serious objective in experi-
menting with words than the delight which this afforded. She was concerned with language as an instrument for communication. Her capacity
to perceive the significant and her desire to express her perceptions in
poetic form made this concern inevitable. To a mind brimming with
acute impressions, observations, and speculations, the ambiguity of ordinary language must have seemed intolerable. The evidence is clear

[19] *Poems,* p. 178, No. xlviii.
[20] *Ibid.,* p. 159, No. v.
[21] *Ibid.,* p. 201, No. c.
[22] *Ibid.,* p. 425, No. lxxxii.

that she gave great care to the evaluation of not only lines but the very syllables of each word. In this way she apparently hoped to achieve a skill in the use of language which would preclude ambiguity and verbosity. Hypothetically, we can trace the reasoning which led her to her unique way of using words.

The tendency of human minds to interpret words in the light of their own prejudices, ignorances, and inclinations is easily apparent. Therefore the fewer words one used, the less opportunity he provided for misinterpretation—that is, if the words were chosen which in their denotative meanings and their connotative associations would most exactly convey one's intentions. Thus Emily Dickinson attempted to develop a shorthand system of poetic language which would combine the advantage of conciseness with the capability of connoting a rich complex of suggestions.

In conjunction with the development of a shorthand language arose an unshakable attachment to *frugality, economy, conciseness, reticence,* and *simplicity.* Any reader of the Dickinson poems will recognize these concepts as typical and often recurring themes. One suspects that she admired frugality not only for its usefulness in poetic communication but also as a compelling concept in itself. At any rate, her poems show *economy* to have been a constant watchword. Even a rat is described as having "concise" characteristics and as being "a foe so reticent." [23] Valuable or awesome things—books, lover's words, nature, death—are all described in terms of frugality, simplicity, and reticence.[24] The human being in particular achieved stature and power in proportion to his reserve.

> I fear a man of scanty speech,
> I fear a silent man,
> Haranguer I can overtake
> Or babbler entertain—
>
> But he who waiteth while the rest
> Expend their inmost pound,
> Of this Man I am wary—
> I fear that He is Grand.[25]

She felt, truly enough, that she herself was liberally endowed with the supreme virtue of reticence. In some poems she symbolically identifies her own existence as a form and practice of some type of economy.

[23] *Poems,* p. 84, No. xxxv.
[24] *Ibid.,* p. 46, No. xcix; p. 83, No. xxxi; p. 233, No. xxxiv; and *Bolts of Melody,* p. 192, No. 356.
[25] *Poems,* p. 277, No. i.

> Alone and in a circumstance
> Reluctant to be told,
> A spider on my reticence
> Deliberately crawled . . .[26]

Twice she refers to "my frugal eyes." [27] And the following poem has autobiographical overtones even if she were not specifically talking about herself.

> Superiority to fate
> Is difficult to learn.
> 'Tis not conferred by any,
> But possible to earn
>
> A pittance at a time,
> Until, to her surprise,
> The soul with strict economy
> Subsists till Paradise.[28]

In respect to Emily Dickinson's concept of economy, one can trace the progression of her thinking from a reverence for words to a realization that "scanty speech" is the most effective means of communicating and to an emphasis upon the concept of frugality as a value in itself. "Oneness" is the essence of meaningful experience.

> One and One are One,
> Two be finished using,
> Well enough for schools,
> But for inner choosing,
> Life—just, or Death—
> Or the Everlasting.
> Two would be too vast,
> For the Soul's comprising.[29]

From this position it was inevitable that Emily Dickinson would proceed to the logical conclusion that if economy and reticence of expression were more meaningful than the effusiveness and carelessness of most ordinary speech, then still more significant would be *silence*. This conclusion was apparently her final and unwavering position in regard to the efficacy of words and became one of her most pervasive themes. Two

---

[26] *Bolts of Melody*, p. 102, No. 181.
[27] *Poems*, p. 47, No. cii; and p. 173, No. xxxvi.
[28] *Ibid.*, p. 41, No. lxxv.
[29] *Ibid.*, p. 356, No. cxl.

aspects of her experience supported such a conviction and probably contributed to its genesis.

First she saw that the most awe-inspiring and significant things experienced in the external world are wrapped in silence and mystery.

> Aloud
> Is nothing that is chief,
> But still.[30]

Faced with this fact, Emily Dickinson could only adopt a "reverential face" and, in her idiom, not profane the time with the symbol of a word.[31]

> My best acquaintances are those
> With whom I spoke no word;
> The stars that stated come to town
> Esteemed me never rude
>
> Although to their celestial call
> I failed to make reply,
> My constant reverential face
> Sufficient courtesy.[32]

The essential element in this poem is Emily Dickinson's avowal that non-speaking, inanimate "things" are her best acquaintances. In this category would fall the sublime aspects of nature such as the volcano:

> The reticent volcano keeps
>   His never slumbering plan;
> Confided are his projects pink
>   To no precarious man.[33]

And the sea which

> Develops pearl and weed,
> But only to himself is known
> The fathoms they abide.[34]

[30] *Bolts of Melody,* p. 249, No. 485.
[31] *Poems,* p. 133, No. xiii.
[32] *Bolts of Melody,* p. 122, No. 225.
[33] *Poems,* p. 49, No. cvii.
[34] *Ibid.,* p. 136, No. xvii.

And Nature as a total phenomenon:

> We pass and she abides;
> We conjugate her skill
> While she creates and federates
> Without a syllable.[35]
>
> Nature is what we know
> But have no art to say,
> So impotent our wisdom is
> To Her simplicity.[36]

Emily Dickinson's "best acquaintances" also included such intangible concepts as Melody:

> The definition of melody is
> That definition is none.[37]

Life:

> A still volcano—Life—
> That flickered in the night
> When it was dark enough to show
> Without endangering sight.[38]

the Future:

> The Future never spoke,
> Nor will he, like the Dumb,
> Reveal by sign or syllable
> Of his profound To-come.[39]

Divinity:

> Divinity dwells under the seal.[40]

or God:

> Our little secrets slink away
> Beside God's "will not tell" . . .[41]

[35] *Bolts of Melody*, p. 51, No. 92.
[36] *Poems*, p. 233, No. xxxiv.
[37] *Ibid.*, p. 310, No. lvii.
[38] *Ibid.*, p. 292, No. xxxiii.
[39] *Ibid.*, p. 232, No. xxxi.
[40] *Bolts of Melody*, p. 249, No. 485.
[41] *Ibid.*, p. 280, No. 560.

the Heavens:

> The Heavens with a smile
> Sweep by our disappointed heads,
> But deign no syllable.[42]

and of course—Death:

> The Living tell
> The Dying but a syllable;
> The coy Dead—none.[43]

> Like Death,
>   Who only shows his
>   Marble disc—
> Sublimer sort than speech.[44]

All these "best acquaintances" have in common the characteristic, extremely significant for Emily Dickinson, of existing on levels incomprehensible to the human mind, of never yielding the secret of their nature. As I have already observed, Emily Dickinson probably concluded that the withdrawal from communication manifested by the mightiest things conceivable to the human mind was worth emulating, in so far as possible, by the mightiest human minds.

The second aspect of her experience which led her to a worshipful attitude toward silence was her intimate knowledge of human experience. She, perhaps as much as any other human being, was aware of the profound complexities of experience which accompany, like the submerged mass of an iceberg, the apparent superficiality and simplicity of daily life. These complexities, she knew, defined the limits of communication and made inevitable the fact that the essential nature of human beings must always remain secreted in the lonely isolation of the individual.

> Growth of Man like growth of Nature
> Gravitates within,
> Atmosphere and sun confirm it
> But it stirs alone.

> Each its difficult ideal
> Must achieve itself,

---

[42] *Poems*, p. 321, No. lxxx.
[43] *Ibid.*, p. 447, No. cxvii.
[44] *Poems*, p. 271, No. cxlii.

> Through the solitary prowess
> Of a silent life.[45]

Emily Dickinson noticed that it was the most significant aspects of the human being which seemed most removed from communication.

> Best things dwell out of sight—
> The pearl, the just, our thought . . .[46]

> Speech is a symptom of affection,
> And Silence one,
> The perfectest communication
> Is heard of none . . .[47]

Of the two symptoms of affection Emily Dickinson's preference is clearly for silence—not an empty, passive silence but one made electric by the energy of a powerful restraint.

> There is no silence in the earth so silent
>   As that endured
> Which, uttered, would discourage nature
> And haunt the world.[48]

The significance of silence is not comprised in a lack of something but in a tremendous excess existing within the human being. Extremes of emotion such as joy or grief, for instance, often underlie a meaningful silence. Emily Dickinson knew from her own experience that verbalization is hopelessly inadequate beyond a certain point to express joy:

> If I could tell how glad I was,
> I should not be so glad,
> But when I cannot make the Force
> Nor mould it into word,
> I know it is a sign
> That new Dilemma be
> From mathematics further off,
> Than from Eternity.[49]

[45] *Ibid.*, p. 282, No. xiv.
[46] *Bolts of Melody*, p. 274, No. 543.
[47] *Poems*, p. 261, No. cx.
[48] *Bolts of Melody*, p. 250, No. 488.
[49] *Poems*, p. 267, No. cxxviii.

Or grief:

> Best grief is tongueless—[50]

Her observation of other people indicated that the same was true for them.

> Give little anguish
> Lives will fret.
> Give avalanches—
> And they'll slant,
>
> Straighten, look cautious for their breath,
> But make no syllable—
> Like Death,
>   Who only shows his
>   Marble disc—
> Sublimer sort than speech.[51]
>
> The words the happy say
> Are paltry melody;
> But those the silent feel
> Are beautiful.[52]
>
> She was mute from transport,
> I, from agony! [53]

Emily Dickinson asked herself why it was that words, which ordinarily seemed almost infinitely capable of expressing thought and emotion, should on occasion become pitifully inadequate. "Is it that words are suddenly small, or that we are suddenly large, that they cease to suffice us to thank a friend? Perhaps it is chiefly both." [54] Apparently she regarded the expressive power of words and the perceptiveness of the human being as associated in an almost organic relationship. The increase of awareness in a person which made him "suddenly large" was accompanied by an apparent decrease in the effectiveness of words to express the newly acquired excess of thought or emotion. However, even though the deepest thought and emotion dwelled in inexpressible depths, there was, as Emily Dickinson knew, no reason to deny its real existence.

[50] *Bolts of Melody*, p. 252, No. 493.
[51] *Poems*, pp. 270 f., No. cxlii.
[52] *Bolts of Melody*, p. 249, No. 487.
[53] *Poems*, p. 176, No. xlv.
[54] *Letters*, p. 324.

> Gratitude is not the mention
> Of a tenderness,
> But its still appreciation
> Out of plumb of speech.
>
> When the sea return no answer
> By the line and lead
> Proves it there's no sea, or rather
> A remoter bed? [55]

The conclusion, then, to which Emily Dickinson came was that words, powerful as they are, cannot encompass what is truly significant. As a result of this conclusion, her position as a poet who was concerned with molding thought and experience into language was indeed strange. The apparently logical thing to do would be to withdraw from all attempts at language communication and devote herself to a mystical experiencing of truth. Such a course of action would not have been foreign to her nature or inclination. Few persons have so completely withdrawn from human society as she did. However, Emily Dickinson was apparently not the type of person who could attain a completely mystical approach to life. She seemed to feel a desperate need for language communication, or at least the need to organize her experience to such a degree that it could be expressed on paper if only for herself to read. Thus, fully aware that she was attempting the exact thing which she considered impossible, she tried to find phrases for her thoughts.

> I found the phrase to every thought
> I ever had, but one;
> And that defies me,—as a hand
> Did try to chalk the sun
>
> To races nurtured in the dark;—
> How would your own begin?
> Can blaze be done in cochineal,
> Or noon in mazarin? [56]

This poem usually is interpreted as expressing Emily Dickinson's extreme confidence in her ability to express everything except perhaps the concept of immortality. And of course it is evident that she did possess great self-confidence in the use of words; however, this one poem should not make us forget her conviction, expressed repeatedly, that the truly significant things in human experience dwelled in the realm of silence

[55] Bingham, "Poems of Emily Dickinson: Hitherto Published Only in Part," *op. cit.*, p. 38.
[56] *Poems*, p. 17, No. xxxi.

and secrecy. The poem quoted above, furthermore, is not so much a contradiction as a confirmation of her position regarding the impotency of words. In the first place she is speaking of a specific, significant thought—most likely the concept of immortality which she habitually describes in terms of *blaze, noon, sun.* To emphasize the gigantic stature and inaccessibility of this concept, she uses a contrast based upon the clearest, most concise distinction possible—a sharp dichotomy between the concept of immortality and all other concepts. The poem would lose much of its directness and power if she had made a general statement to the effect that she had difficulty expressing the thoughts which concerned her most. Secondly, the exaggeration in the first two lines is too apparent to be taken as literal truth. The one thought she could not express should be considered a symbol of the realm of thoughts which are too intrinsically a part of the human soul to be severed from it. Since such a realm of thoughts would naturally be associated with and probably epitomized by the concept of immortality, it was logical for Emily Dickinson to think of it as the representative "one" thought to which she could not find a phrase. Her desire to be concise, specific, and economic in poetry would inevitably lead her to this solution of a poetic problem.

I have shown how Emily Dickinson's attitude toward words was something of a paradox. Her intellect and intuitive imagination told her that human communication was unavailing before the greatness of the universe and the complexity of man's experience within it. But her emotional nature, her delight in a struggle, and her unlimited courage bade her make the attempt regardless of its futility. As long as her poetry could at least suggest the infiniteness and wonder of the universe, she thought the effort was justified. And if nothing else, she could vividly call attention to poetry's inadequacy for the most significant communication by, paradoxically enough, communicating that very idea as profoundly as she could to any possible reader of her poems. Thus the awe-inspiring mysteries with which Emily Dickinson was concerned would be dramatically focused in the reader's mind through a striking incongruity: powerful poems confessing their powerlessness. The paradox inherent in such a situation is the result of the poet's attempt to bridge the gap between a mortal and superhuman consciousness.

It should be noted that Emily Dickinson did not regard the impotency of words as a total disadvantage. There was an attraction, even a fascination, in the imperfection of human language, for if communication was necessarily incomplete and vague, the human imagination was thus allowed more scope, given more importance, and developed more extensively. All poets by the nature of their calling depend upon and revere the imagination, and Emily Dickinson was no exception. She preferred the world of her own creation to the objective world of observable fact.

The lady in the following poem knows that the "image" has advantages over the "interview."

> A charm invests a face
> Imperfectly beheld,—
> The lady dare not lift her veil
> For fear it be dispelled
>
> But peers beyond her mesh,
> And wishes, and denies,—
> Lest interview annul a want
> That image satisfies.[57]

In another poem on the same theme Emily Dickinson uses erotic imagery in a highly unusual context.

> Did the harebell loose her girdle
> To the lover bee,
> Would the bee the harebell hallow
> Much as formerly?
>
> Did the paradise, persuaded,
> Yield her moat of pearl,
> Would the Eden be an Eden,
> Or the earl an earl? [58]

An image of a maiden who maintains her alluring mystery and attractiveness by preserving her chastity is here applied to a harebell, and then in a daring extension to Heaven itself. Heaven and God, if perceived and understood by men, would not retain their present status in men's thoughts and imagination. The implication is that incommunicableness in this case is a distinct advantage.

[57] *Ibid.*, p. 142, No. xxviii.

[58] *Ibid.*, p. 142, No. xxvii. Richard Chase in *Emily Dickinson* ("The American Men of Letters Series"; New York: William Morrow and Associates, 1951), p. 139, makes the following comments on this poem:

"The poem beginning 'Did the harebell loose her girdle' asks, in terms of a rather confused nature allegory, whether female creatures (the category seems extensive) lose caste by yielding to their lovers, and also whether the lovers lose caste (for 'Eden' read 'the innocent sexuality of women,' and for 'earl' read 'lover'): [Mr. Chase quotes here the second stanza of the poem.] There is no specific idea of sin in this poem. The specification is of status, though the exact kind of status in question is, as frequently happens, not very clear."

Why not accept the obvious meaning of "Eden" and "earl" as Heaven and God? Emily Dickinson frequently used terms of royalty to designate God, and she used the words "Eden," "Paradise," "Heaven," "Eternity" as more or less synonymous. See, for example, *Poems*, p. 191, No. lxxiii, and p. 216, No. cxxxvi; pp. 295 f., No. xxxvii, and pp. 309 f., No. lvii.

Perhaps Emily Dickinson's viewpoint concerning the inadequacy of the word to express the poet's deepest intuitions, and yet the value, notwithstanding, of struggling to express the inexpressible is summed up in the following poem.

> To tell the beauty would decrease,
> To state the Spell demean,
> There is a syllableless sea
> Of which it is the sign.
>
> My will endeavours for its word
> And fails, but entertains
> A rapture as of legacies—
> Of introspective mines.[59]

[59] *Poems*, p. 266, No. cxxiv.

The Poet and the Muse: Poetry as Art

by Thomas H. Johnson

. . . It seems to have been in 1860 that Emily Dickinson made the discovery of herself as a poet and began to develop a professional interest in poetic techniques. Her thoughts about poetry and the function of the poet can be gleaned from her own poems and from occasional snatches in her letters. Her writing techniques were self-taught. She did not follow traditional theories, but developed her own along highly original lines. Though she could write excellent prose, easy, clear, unmannered, the fact is that she thought in poetry. By 1858, at ease with the way of life she had elected and found congenial, she had begun to let the form of her verse derive from the images and sensations that she wished to realize. Her growth as an artist can be followed by way of her experiments in prosody. She worked steadily at her trade during 1860 and 1861, and by 1862, when she feared that the loss of her muse would overwhelm her, she had mastered her craft.

Although writers of free verse acknowledge a debt to Emily Dickinson, she wrote in fact almost nothing which today would be called *vers libre,* that is, cadenced verse, as distinguished from that which is metrical or rhymed. Her first attempt to do so in 1862, "Victory comes late," seems to have been her last, for it evidently convinced her that such a form was not the medium which best transmitted her mood and ideas. There are a variety of ways to gain controlled liberty. She herself, she felt, needed rhyme and meter. To her contemporaries, and to most critics at the time her poems were first published, her seemingly unpatterned verses appeared to be the work of an orginal but undisciplined artist. Actually she was creating a new medium of poetic expression.

Basically all her poems employ meters derived from English hymnology. They are usually iambic or trochaic, but occasionally dactylic. They were the metric forms familiar to her from childhood as the measures in which Watts's hymns were composed. Copies of Watts's *Christian Psalmody* or his collection of *The Psalms, Hymns, and Spiritual Songs*

"The Poet and the Muse: Poetry as Art." From *Emily Dickinson: An Interpretive Biography* (Cambridge, Mass.: The Belknap Press of Harvard University Press, 1955) by Thomas Herbert Johnson. Copyright © 1955 by The President and Fellows of Harvard College. Reprinted by permission of the publisher.

were fixtures in every New England household. Both were owned by Edward Dickinson and are inscribed with his name. The latter is bound in brown sheepskin, and bears his name in gold on the cover. Musical notations for proper rendition accompany each song, and the meter is always named. Introductions set forth an explanation of how effects may best be achieved, and discuss the relative advantage of one meter over another for particular occasions. Emily Dickinson's own experimentation went beyond anything envisioned by the formal precisionists who edited Watts's hymns and songs, but the interesting point is that she did not have to step outside her father's library to receive a beginner's lesson in metrics.

The principal iambic meters are these: *Common Meter,* alternately eight and six syllables to the line; *Long Meter,* eight syllables to the line; and *Short Meter,* two lines of six syllables, followed by one of eight, then one of six. Each of these meters has properly four lines to the stanza, so that their syllabic scheme goes thus: *CM,* 8, 6, 8, 6; *LM,* 8, 8, 8, 8; *SM,* 6, 6, 8, 6. Each may also be doubled in length to make eight-line stanzas. Each may also have six lines to the stanza. Thus *Common Particular Meter* has the metric beat 8, 8, 6, 8, 8, 6; and *Short Particular Meter,* 6, 6, 8, 6, 6, 8. Other popular arrangements were *Sevens and Sixes* (7, 6, 7, 6) and *Sixes.* The principal trochaic meters are *Sevens, Eights and Sevens, Eights and Fives, Sevens and Fives, Sixes and Fives,* and *Sixes.* Of the dactyls, which were arranged principally in *Elevens, Elevens and Tens,* and *Tens and Nines,* Emily Dickinson used almost exclusively the last named when she chose it as the meter for an entire poem. But she used the dactyl sparingly and almost always as an adjunct to one of the other meters.

It is significant that every poem she composed before 1861—during the years she was learning her craft—is fashioned in one or another of the hymn meters named above. Her use of Long Meter was sparing, for, as her hymn-book instructions pointed out, it tends to monotony. A very large proportion of her poems are in Common Meter. Next in order are Common Particular, and Sevens and Sixes, in equal proportion. She chose Short Meter for relatively few, but achieved with it some of her best effects. Her trochaics are chiefly Eights and Sevens, and Eights and Fives—a new meter, introduced into hymnody toward the mid-nineteenth century.

The meters so far named by no means exhaust the variations that hymnodists were coming to use, but one need not believe that Emily Dickinson's later combinations of Nines and Sixes, Nines and Fours, or Sixes and Fours derived from a model. By the time she came to use them she was striking out for herself. Indeed her techniques would be of scant interest had she set down her stanzas with the metric regularity of her models, and enforced her rhymes with like exactness. Her great contribution to English prosody was that she perceived how to gain new effects by exploring the possibilities within traditional metric patterns. She then took the final step toward that flexibility within patterns which she sought. She began merging in one poem the various meters themselves so that the forms, which intrinsically carry their own retardment or acceleration, could be made to supply the continuum for the mood and ideas of the language. Thus iambs shift to trochees, trochees to dactyls, and on occasion all three are merged.

At the same time she put into practice her evident belief that verse which limits itself to exact rhyme is denied the possible enrichment that other kinds can bring. Her pioneering is here too in the new order erected on old foundations. She felt no more bound to one kind of rhyme than she did to one meter. She should have realized that she was charting a lonely voyage, and in some degree she did, but her independent nature gave her self-assurance. Her way of poetry was to prove far lonelier than she expected, for it denied her in her own lifetime all public recognition. The metric innovations might have been tolerated, but in her day no critic of English verse would have been willing to accept her rhymes. Milton had proved that English verse could be great with no rhyme at all. No one in 1860, reader or critic, was ready to let it be supple and varied.

Custom decreed exact patterns and exact rhymes in English poetry, with concessions to a spare use of eye rhymes (*come-home*). Her grounding in French and in classical literature, however elementary or imperfect, must have assured her that English custom had no preemptive sanction. She enormously extended the range of variation within controlled limits by adding to exact and eye rhymes four types that poets writing in English had never learned to use expertly enough to gain for them a general acceptance: identical rhymes (*move-remove*), vowel rhymes (*see-buy*), imperfect rhymes [identical vowels followed by different consonants] (*time-thine*), and suspended rhyme [different vowels followed by identical consonants] (*thing-along*). These rhymes she selected at will, singly or in combination, and she carried her freedom to the utmost limit by feeling no compulsion to use one rhyming pattern in a poem any more than she felt constrained to use a single metric form. Thus in a poem of three quatrains the rhyme in the first stanza may be exact for the second and fourth lines, suspended in the second stanza for lines three and four, and conclude in the third stanza with imperfect rhymes for the first and fourth lines. The wheel horses of her stanzas are always the final lines, whether the poem is written as a series of quatrains or as a combination of stanza patterns.

Within this structure she was seldom wayward, nor did she have to be, for it gave her ample room for variety of mood, speed, and circuit. Examination of the intent of a poem usually reveals a motive for the variations. Sometimes she seems to have felt, as the reader does today, that a poem was unskillfully realized, for she abandoned a great many such efforts in worksheet draft. In the past editors have published her finished poems side by side with texts created from unfinished worksheets. Thus imperfectly realized poems have been given a status which the poet never thought them to have. The level of the poet's achievement is raised when such unfinished labors are not weighed in.

One of the very earliest poems to adopt combinations of patterns is the following, written in 1858.

> I never told the buried gold
> Upon the hill—that lies—
> I saw the sun—his plunder done
> Crouch low to guard his prize.
>
> He stood as near
> As stood you here—
> A pace had been between—
> Did but a snake bisect the brake
> My life had forfeit been.
>
> That was a wondrous booty—
> I hope twas honest gained.
> Those were the fairest ingots
> That ever kissed the spade!
>
> Whether to keep the secret—
> Whether to reveal—
> Whether as I ponder
> "Kidd" will sudden sail—
>
> Could a shrewd advise me
> We might e'en divide—
> Should a shrewd betray me—
> Atropos decide!

The metric and rhyme shifts are many and seem to be deliberate. The first two stanzas, in Common Meter, are followed by a third in Sevens and Sixes. The fourth, beginning in line two, shifts to trochaic Sixes and Fives, with which the poem concludes in stanza five. The rhymes are exact in the first, second, and last stanzas; imperfect in the third, and suspended in the fourth. There are internal exact rhymes in the first and third lines of stanzas one and two. The poem survives in two fair copies, and in both she has deliberately arranged the second stanza in five lines.

The variations are studied and so elaborate that they distract the reader. She appears to be describing a brilliant sunset, and is undecided whether to share the "secret" or not. The structural form when she narrates the facts of the event is exact in meter and rhyme. Both shift uncertainly as she points out her own indecision. It is not an important poem. The imagery is imprecise and the intent not clearly realized. The poet is still a tyro, but such skill as the poem has—and unmistakably it bears her stamp—lies in the blending of the form with the mood.

The poem below, also written in 1858, is an accomplishment of the first order. The skills she was developing are more easily handled in two quatrains than in five.

> I never lost as much but twice,
> And that was in the sod.
> Twice have I stood a beggar
> Before the door of God!
>
> Angels—twice descending
> Reimbursed my store—
> Burglar! Banker—Father!
> I am poor once more!

The first stanza is written in Common Meter with a catalectic third line— that is, it lacks a final syllable. The device was one that she developed with uncanny skill to break the monotony of exact regularity. The second stanza is a trochee in Sixes and Fives. Here the metric irregularity is balanced by exact rhymes. The exactness of the rhymes gives finality to the terseness of the thought. The metrical shift turns the resignation of the first statement into the urgency of the second.

Sometime about 1860 she wrote this:

> Just lost, when I was saved!
> Just felt the world go by!
> Just girt me for the onset with Eternity,
> When breath blew back,
> And on the other side
> I heard recede the disappointed tide!
>
> Therefore, as One returned, I feel,
> Odd secrets of the line to tell!
> Some Sailor, skirting foreign shores—
> Some pale Reporter, from the awful doors
> Before the Seal!
>
> Next time, to stay!
> Next time, the things to see
> By Ear unheard,
> Unscrutinized by Eye—

> Next time, to tarry,
> While the Ages steal—
> Slow tramp the Centuries,
> And the Cycles wheel!

It is arranged in several metric patterns, altered so rapidly that no single form predominates. The final short stanza alternates iambs with trochees, to give the effect of applying brakes, and thus brings the slow tramp of the centuries to a halt. The final words of each stanza effect a rhyme, and most of the rhymes are exact. In the first stanza the mating rhyme word is in the line preceding, and in the second it is separated by three intervening lines. In the last two stanzas it is at the point normally expected, that is, in the alternating line. There are further rhymes in the first two stanzas, exact, vowel, and suspended. This elaborateness is shaped throughout to the mood the poem intends to convey, a mood of awe in facing the fact that any vision of immortality seen by mortals is a mirage. The structure of the poem allows great latitude in tempo and shading. The poem is one of her best early attempts to create by way of letting the form be shaped by the mood. The method requires a skill which cannot be taught, but must be guided by instinctive taste. She herself did not win through to full success on all occasions. But the universal pleasure this poem has given is some measure of its fulfillment.

A very large number of poems written during 1860 and 1861 experiment with new models. She used much the same technique as that in the poem above when she created "At last, to be identified," evidently with intent likewise to suggest breathlessness. In 1860 she also wrote the expertly realized "How many times these low feet staggered." It is the quiet meditation of one who gazes upon the face and form of a dead friend. The metrics are coldly regular. The hovering rhyme of the first stanza becomes exact in the remaining two stanzas. The artistry lies in the vivid concreteness of the detail, set forth with great restraint. On the privacy of this moment no rhetorical extravagance is allowed to obtrude.

The new order of love poems is exemplified by this.

> I'm 'wife'—I've finished that—
> That other state—
> I'm Czar—I'm 'Woman' now—
> It's safer so—
>
> How odd the Girl's life looks
> Behind this soft Eclipse—
> I think that Earth feels so
> To folks in Heaven—now—

> This being comfort—then
> That other kind—was pain—
> But why compare?
> I'm 'Wife'! Stop there!

Suspended rhymes join each pair of lines except the last, which conclude the poem with exact rhymes. Each stanza has its individual metric form, allied to but not identical with the others. The Sixes and Fours of the first stanza become Sixes in the second. In the third, the Sixes are paired, as are the Fours.

The rhythmic exactness of "Did the Harebell loose her girdle/To the Lover bee" is as studied as the irregularity in "What is 'Heaven,'" written at the same time. The poem below is an excellent example of both her concern with and indifference to rhyme and metrical exactness.

> I taste a liquor never brewed—
> From Tankards scooped in Pearl—
> Not all the Frankfort Berries
> Yield such an Alcohol!
>
> Inebriate of Air—am I—
> And Debauchee of Dew—
> Reeling—thro endless summer days—
> From inns of Molten Blue—
>
> When "Landlords" turn the drunken Bee
> Out of the Foxglove's door—
> When Butterflies—renounce their "drams"—
> I shall but drink the more!
>
> Till Seraphs swing their snowy Hats—
> And Saints—to windows run—
> To see the little Tippler
> From Manzanilla come!

The poem uses Common Meter, but the regularity is broken in two ways. The third lines of the first and fourth stanzas are both catalectic, and the rhymes of those stanzas are imperfect. These variations unquestionably were deliberate, for they are typical of her modifications of traditional forms. Yet the only surviving manuscript of the poem is a semifinal draft on which she offers alternative readings for two lines. For line three she suggests: "Not all the vats upon the Rhine," and for the final line: "Leaning against the sun." The first alternative, if adopted, would supply the missing half-foot; the second would create an exact rhyme. We cannot infer from the fact that the suggested changes exist that she would have adopted them in a fair copy. She frequently did not do so. There are instances where two fair copies, each sent to a friend, show like indifference to rhyme and metric patterns. One may hazard the opinion that her choice in any event would have been determined by her preference for one image rather than another, not by a desire to create exact meter and rhyme.

She must have been groping too for ways of expression that said things as she individually wished to say them. Certain of her idiosyncrasies in language and grammar become obtrusive when sprinkled too freely, but they are characteristic and often very effective. Her use of what seems to be the subjunctive mood comes first to mind. Yet the fact is that perhaps it is not subjunctive at all in the sense of being grammatically an optative or volitive or potential mood. "Only love assist the wound" may be read as "Only love can assist the wound." But more probably, because more in line with the way her mind worked, she means "Only love does assist the wound." If this is her meaning, then what at first seems to be a subjunctive mood might better be called a continuing or universal present indicative. She recognized her dilemma in the line "Beauty—be not caused—It Is." As a suggested change she offers "is" for "be," as though she were uncertain whether the substantive sense was too unidiomatic to convey her idea clearly. But even the first reading cannot be called subjunctive, for it does not denote a contingency, but expresses an idea as fact. She was trying to universalize her thought to embrace past, present, and future. Such is her intent in the following instances, which could be multiplied greatly, so often does her mind explore universals.

> Nature—the Gentlest Mother is . . .
> And when the Sun go down—
> Her Voice among the Aisles
> Incite the timid prayer

> The One who could repeat the Summer Day . . .
> When Orient have been outgrown—
> And Occident—become Unknown—
> His Name—remain—

> The Robin is the One
> That interrupt the Morn

This concept of language is allied to but different from that which prompted her to cultivate elliptical phrases as a way of paring words that complete sentences grammatically but do not communicate. Of course on occasion she cut too deeply into the quick of her thought because she truncated her predication to the point where readers must perpetually grope for meaning. But where her intent is realized, the attar becomes haunting and unforgettable. . . .

Emily Dickinson's Notation

by R. P. Blackmur

Some twenty years ago it was necessary to begin an essay on Emily
Dickinson with a complaint that the manuscripts and the various copies
of manuscripts of this poet had never been adequately edited, and could
never be properly read until they were. It seems to me now—and the
reviews I have seen agree—that Mr. Johnson has done everything an
editor can do,[1] and that there remains—and on this Mr. Johnson himself insists in his preface—the second task of providing a more readable,
and less expensive, edition for the ordinary purposes of poetry. This I
hope Mr. Johnson will undertake because, whoever undertakes it, it
will be the completion of Mr. Johnson's own work; and because it will
itself be a criticism of Emily Dickinson's work at almost every possible
level. The principal problem, it seems to me, will be to find within the
general conventions of printing a style of presentation which will furnish
a version conformable to the original notation which the poet employed.
The Dickinson practice was to punctuate by dashes, as if the reader
would know what the dashes meant—both grammatically and dramatically—by giving the verses voice. Within her practice, and to her
own ear, she was no doubt consistent. To find out what that consistency
was, and to articulate it for other readers and other voices, requires more
of a system than ever bothered her. Even a casual examination of any
twenty pages in this new edition makes this aspect of the problem plain.
Here is an example to do for the rest.

> Some—work for Immortality—
> The chiefer part, for Time—
> He—Compensates—immediately—
> The former—Checks—on Fame—

"Emily Dickinson's Notation," by R. P. Blackmur. From *The Kenyon Review* Vol.
18 (Spring 1956). Copyright © 1956 by *The Kenyon Review*. Reprinted by permission
of the author and *The Kenyon Review*.

[1] *The Poems of Emily Dickinson.* "Including variant readings critically compared
with all known manuscripts." Edited by Thomas H. Johnson. The Belknap Press of
Harvard University Press.

Emily Dickinson. An Interpretive Biography. By Thomas H. Johnson. The Belknap
Press of Harvard University Press.

The Dickinson practice cannot be systematized; there is not enough *there;* but with enough intimacy with the poems we can see what sort of system might have emerged. The problem is not very different, so I understand, in reading the official prose of Japan in 1865; but in English poetry it seldom presents itself with such multiplicity of irritation—so much freedom in rearrangement—with such spontaneity left to the reader.

Multiplicity, freedom, spontaneity: these are terms for much deeper aspects of the Dickinson notation than that which gathers itself in mere punctuation, syntax and grammar; or in meter, rhythm, and diction. Perhaps the deepest problem in poetics raises one of its prettiest examples in her notation. How much does a poet look to words to supply what is put down, and how much to notate what was within the self prior to the words? If words are necessarily the medium of poetry, how much do they also participate in its substance? If thought looks for words as a chief medium for turning it into action, how much, if anything, of the action is in the movement of the words themselves? Is there not in the end a nearly equal contest between the thought prior to the words and the thought already reminiscent in the words and their arrangements? If so, victory for the poem will be in the equilibrium between the two; what is in W. B. Cannon's physiology the maintenance of a precarious stable state, or homeostasis, called the wisdom of the body. This equilibrium, this wisdom, is in poetry recorded, though it is not maintained; is communicated, though it does not exist—in the words taken as notation. In this respect the words resemble the notes in music.

The words resemble the notes on the musical score. This is not said as a triviality but as a fact about poetry and music which no theory can ultimately ignore. It is said that Beethoven sometimes wrote out his initial score in words, and surely there are some poems where the words seem like the notes in a final score—as perhaps "The Phoenix and the Turtle." There is only a difference in the degree of notation. The point is that the notation is always inadequate, by itself, in predicting performance or reading. As the poet was saying much more, so the reader is left with more or less to do for himself as the notation wills him or fails him. This is why the poem which has seemed flat will spring into life when one has got intimate with that will. My friends the composers tell me that the notation in music is perhaps eighty-five per cent adequate, which seems to me high and can only be true of modern music (the music the composers themselves wrote). In poetry I am convinced the notation is at best only about fifteen per cent adequate for a full reading; the gaps jumped are *that* much greater; and indeed a single reading can never again be more than approximately repeated, and as the approximations go on, the life of the poem thickens in the reader's mind and throat. The uniqueness of each reading reaches towards the uniqueness of the poem. Thus the poet's own reading, like his own notation, is often inadequate to the poem; his voice no more than his words is not up to a final job, but yet always should be heard. We cannot do without as much of the feasible fifteen per cent as we can get from the poet or can, after sufficient intimacy, otherwise arrange for. In Emily Dickinson's case the notation in the words seldom reaches the feasible maximum even with intimacy; and it is here, I think, that the final problem of critical editorship lies, since we must not permit ourselves to lose the record of our intimacy. The editor must learn to notate the voice which in intimacy he has learned to hear; which is not at all the same thing as notating merely what he has learned to understand. Consider why Toscanini is a great conductor, and then consider how Emily Dickinson's poems, all short, have none of the self-modulating advantages of length or any of the certainties of complex overt structure. One exaggerates, but it sometimes seems as if in her work a cat came at us speaking English, our own language, but without the pressure of all the other structures we are accustomed to attend; it comes at us all voice so far as it is in control, fragmented elsewhere, willful and arbitrary, because it has not the acknowledged means to be otherwise.

All this Mr. Johnson's edition makes plain, and makes it plain not only about the extreme case (which as in fever is only a degree or so) of Emily Dickinson, which would be merely to dismiss her, but about a great deal and to some extent all of poetry, which is why more than ever we would save her in spite of all her losses incurred on her own account. His own effort in this direction, which I hope will reach to a critical canon of the poems at their maximum potential of notation, is so far to be found in his interpretive biography; and it is with this book and its notations, and what happens to them in my mind, that the remainder of these notes will mainly concern themselves. To begin with there is more sense in his biography, and more nonsense left out, than in any of the other biographies or studies I have read. It may be that he has avoided some real problems of personal relation, but it is certain that he has obviated a good many artificial problems and mere traps of possibility. If he does not speculate about the direction or the substance of her eroticism, he allows, and even encourages, the facts which he exhibits to speculate for themselves: as we do in all our intimate interests which do not transgress themselves in gossip. Mr. Johnson is concerned in both his edition and his biography with establishing Emily Dickinson's identity and the evidences of form that declare it. In the edition the relations are made to speak entirely for themselves as they are spread seriatim and according to a chronological spirit; in the biography the relations are grouped irregularly with regard to chronology and to theme, and so are helped to speak for themselves more clearly in our tongue. Yet identity is always a mystery—precisely the mystery in others that is beyond us the more we share it; and as I become more familiar with the outlines of Mr. Johnson's figure of identity, I find myself encouraged to speculate or contemplate a little the intimations I feel. There is nothing in Mr. Johnson that would make me alter the judgment I found rising from the reading of the poems twenty years ago, but there is a great deal that would suggest deepening that judgment which is the acknowledgment of identity. There is more in Emily Dickinson of the same sort than I had seen; she has more *semblables* and perhaps less, or a different, *vraisemblance*. So one speculates.

I see in the looking-glass how much she is a nuptial poet, and I think of her in connection with two other poets who might also be called nuptial poets, Robert Herrick and Rainer Maria Rilke. I speak of course of the poetry. All three celebrate the kind of intimacy we celebrate and sometimes find as nuptial. Herrick marries the created world; Emily Dickinson marries herself. Rilke creates within himself something to marry which will—which does—marry and thereby rival the real world. Each marriage is an effort towards identity—by acceptance, by withdrawal, by rivalry in all three, but with the emphases different in each. Let us throw these up one by one with deliberate exaggeration.

In Herrick, one spends all one's life in returning from the withdrawal (the splitting off from the general) accomplished by a particular birth. The formality of verse, and the wonderful superficial experimentation around the norm of verse, and the formality of attitude, and the sensuality of both, are means of bridging gaps, are helps in anticipation of gaps, and are projections or hypotheses of particular experience—where the direct experience remains only in detail. It is as if, in Herrick's mind, the direct experience was accepted only for the sake of something else which was to be found in the plenitude of God's creation of nature. Thus it is that the clergyman wore the sexual garment sweet. He played at wearing great costumes in which we acknowledge the union of God and Nature, he played at casting himself in what roles he could of all those which God provided. I think particularly of "A Nuptiall Song on Sir Clipseby Crew and His Lady." Herrick's order is the world's order of his time, his poetry what he did with that order with his senses and with his forms. It is elegance taking flesh.

In Emily Dickinson, one spends all one's life finding a role apart from life, an outer role within which one creates one's own role in spite of (and thereby counselled by) the world. Born in unity, one cuts oneself off, and cuts one's losses in the role of one's own immortality. What was sensuality in Herrick becomes in Emily Dickinson the flow of deprived sensation on the quick. In her, direct experience (often invented, sometimes originally contingent) was always for the sake of something else which would replace the habit and the destructive gusto (but not the need) of experience in the world, and become an experience of its own on its own warrant and across a safe or forbidding gap. This is the best that can be done with the puerile marriage of the self with the self—like the sanctity of the puerile saints in William James: a sensorium for the most part without

the senses, it is sometimes the vision of sense itself. Emily Dickinson withdrew from the world in all the ways she could manage, and was connected with the world by the *pangs* of the experience she could not abide
and yet could not let go. She could not perfect her withdrawal, and she
found herself in successive stages of the inability to return. She had the
experience of withdrawal without return; she found herself a shut-in,
which was the best she could do with finding herself in the beginning a
shut-out. Hence the basic formality and loose form of her common meters
—her hymn forms which do not become hymns; it is the oldest form of
English verse, but is very seldom long used by great poets, though often
used a little. Hence, too, the wilfulness of her syntax led to irregularities
rather than to new orders, which would have compelled at least a formal
return. One thinks in her of enthusiastic transcendence and of lyric
solipsism. Her disorder is her own. Also, which is more significant, her
order is almost only her own. She withdrew from both the disorder of the
outer world in experience and the outer world of order in reason. It was
as if she was afraid to pay attention to what is contingent and embarrassing and scandalous—to what is pressing—either in sensation or pre-
dilection in the experience either of people or of the orders people make
of their impulses in order to get along with their behavior. I do not say
she did this except exemplarily in her conduct, but that under the theory
of life that is in them this is what she did in her poems. Thus she made
the poems of a withdrawal without a return: a withdrawal into spontaneity not experience. All her life she was looking for a subject, and the
looking *was* her subject—in life as in poetry.

> Elysium is as far as to
> The very nearest Room
> If in that Room a Friend await
> Felicity or Doom—
>
> What fortitude the Soul contains,
> That it can so endure
> The accent of a coming Foot—
> The opening of a Door—   (#1760)

She was not the watcher; she looked only for a focus without having a
target—since the target was to *have*. This is sometimes called looking
for frustrations, but in this poet it amounted to a means of making poems.
There was no mountain of refuge and also no mountain of fall. She said
of herself, when "someone rang the bell . . . I ran, as is my custom."
Colonel Higginson wrote to his wife when he first met Emily Dickinson: "I never was with anyone who drained my nerve power so much.
Without touching her, she drew from me. I am glad not to live near her."
Thus she both drained and was drained by others. Mr. Johnson remarks
that "the idea of an affection which in the presence of friends gives way

to panic made her feel guilty." It is as if she got, at the quick, the sense of vampirage which is usually only a possible accompaniment of relation, but which is yet one of the excesses to which the soul is prone: as we see in Henry James, where it is the fate of people who know each other well to destroy each other. This is why to both James and Emily Dickinson renunciation is the "piercing" virtue. It is why, in Emily Dickinson's soul, there was something that kept her from going to church. Of a preacher she writes, "He fumbles at your soul," then

> Deals—One—imperial—Thunderbolt—
> That scalps your naked Soul—

Here her words get ahead of—or come ahead of—and create her intuition, just as in another version of the same intuition (#501) the words lag a little:

> Narcotics cannot still the Tooth
> That nibbles at the soul—

If in Herrick one spends one's life in returning, and in Dickinson in perfecting it, in Rilke one spends all one's life in a constant succession (almost simultaneous in experience) of withdrawal and return: withdrawal from the actual world and return to the same world, with no loss of response to it, but with something added to that world in the sense he made of it. Rilke built his own death, and made all the world of it; and so he built his own life also. This he had to do because life—God's creation of it alone—had lost its plenitude, its habit of continuing creation. In Rilke, it is the chain of being that is our own, the plenitude is for us to find in order to make the chain great. This is the pull in Rilke that makes him great as a poet: he makes that sense, and draws us after. His order is his own, and we use it in our own order. Dickinson we use when we have none. In Dickinson there is the *terribilità* of our inner escape; in Rilke there is the greater *terribilità* of that impossible act, full assent in natural piety.

Both Rilke and Emily Dickinson were obsessed to create mortal images of immortality. So were Milton and Dante. I do not mean to hit Emily Dickinson over the head with Dante, but merely to remind the reader immediately lost in Dickinson of that other species of image where immortality is so much more enlivening than in Dickinson that a different part of our being quivers in response to it. Yet it is a part of what Dickinson depended on. Here is the end of the sonnet that begins *Tanto gentile e tanto onesta.*

> E par che de la sua labbia si mova
> un spirito soave e pien d'amore,
> che va dicendo a l'anima: Sospira.

Here is the best that Emily Dickinson can do in her analogous line—and it is very good. I wish more to point out what is different rather than what is missing.

> All Circumstances are the Frame
> In which His Face is set—
> All Latitudes exist for His
> Sufficient Continent—
>
> The Light His Action, and the Dark
> The Leisure of His Will—
> In Him Existence serve or Set
> A Force illegible.

In the "Dark Leisure of His Will" squirms the protestant, than whom nobody could have been more so—because more *manqué*—than Emily Dickinson. She had protestantism without the business instincts of her contemporaries and without the roast beef of Bunyan and without the secular evangelism of Wesley; she had the resignation and the loneliness and the excruciation—she had the characteristic *misery* of protestantism and a version of her own for its hysterical glee. The soul so inhabited tends to have psychogenic perception only. We like to say that misery, or suffering, matures us to the point where it is impossible to write—and yet one writes, and what one writes has nothing whatever to do with maturity or with immaturity either. Emotions are not susceptible of maturity.

> Rearrange a "Wife's" affection!
> When they dislocate my Brain!
> Amputate my freckled Bosom!
> Make me bearded like a man!
>
> Blush, my spirit, in thy Fastness—
> Blush, my unacknowledged clay—
> Seven years of troth have taught thee
> More than Wifehood ever may!
>
> Love that never leaped its socket—
> Trust entrenched in narrow pain—
> Constancy thro' fire—awarded—
> Anguish—bare of anodyne!
>
> Burden—borne so far triumphant—
> None suspect me of the crown,
> For I wear the "Thorns" till *Sunset*—
> Then—my Diadem put on.

> Big my Secret but it's *bandaged*—
> It will never get away
> Till the Day its Weary Keeper
> Leads it through the Grave to thee. (#1737)

This is not maturity. What we have is a shift of phase (as from ice to steam) in the *verse,* which has its own form of maturity: the form by which one learns to deal with one's persistent adolescence. In Emily Dickinson we seldom see a completely mature verse, though we often see the elements of such a verse. Perhaps we see her own adolescence *and* her own maturity peep through. Both are fragmentary. We cannot say of this woman in white that she ever mastered life—even in loosest metaphor; but we can say that she so dealt with it as to keep it from mastering her —by her protestant self-excruciation in life's name.

It is at this point that in the pursuit of identity, as Mr. Johnson describes it, she did not "clearly find herself" in the excruciation of the lines beginning

> The Missing All—prevented Me
> From missing minor things.

One would rather say that in these lines, so far as they are topical, she found that she had missed herself. In a way—in a verse way, echoing other lines—she made a protection, a carapace of white cotton, even of brocade, so that raw life could not sack the emptiness within. She has all the pang—the expectation, the reversal—of experience without the experience. But for how much the pang may be made to count, to stand, even to *be!*

In making it so count, she is scrupulous; all the little pains of life, the sharp stones in her boots, both those that exist and those that might yet come, or cannot come, spring up and are taken into excruciating account; and there is a strain in universal behavior which needs precisely this account; and poems of this sort are what permit us to bear it. When we read them, as when we write them, we stand incriminated.

The scruple and the incrimination are like those in Gide, a comparison of which it is worth thinking a little, for it shows how Gide is a little too evil in the self-convicted sense, just as Emily Dickinson is a little too good in her sense of badness. Each is tortured by the scruple of the unexpected, what could come to the free act—as if for both, free will were found in action, without motive. Gide was tortured by the inner world of necessary insight, Emily Dickinson was tortured by the outer and frightful world of contingency. Each *gave up that* citadel; which is why Gide had to live so long and in such a hurry to come on himself, where Emily Dickinson had to hurry to die young enough. To keep going, Emily Dickinson had a

resourceful barbarism of the soul which would ally itself with no tradition, where Gide had a resourceful barbarism of conduct. It is in the
exaggerations of our principles that we expose ourselves to the quick and
barb of truth. Each was enthusiastic, protestant (Jansenist or Puritan—in
this respect there is little difference), and each was short on decency to
one's equals, in the nervous drive to bring experience into a form just
short of excruciation. Thus I do not think either of them much of a hand
at discriminating experience; for each was under the mastery of incrimination. *La vie est vraie et criminelle!* cried LaForgue. It is ourselves who
are incriminated, seems to be the thematic statement of Gide and Emily
Dickinson. Hence their cruelty, the one to others, the other to herself.
Hence each is playful in a primitivism, not a maturity, of emotion. Hence
each has the kind of personality which is almost wholly informed by
temperament and makes of it a substitute for sensibility. Yet each is
powerful in reach upon the neighboring forms in our own temperament.

I do not know that the playfulness of Emily Dickinson's temperament
can be illustrated in her verse alone; I am tolerably sure her verse was not
very conscious of it. Yet I think it is there, like the playful ambiguity of
a kitten being a tiger: an ad-libbing of resources of which one is not too
much aware, but which inhabit one at the edge of being. Here one is
very skilful because one has all instinct to bring to bear. Let us look
askance at one of the better known poems, but with an ad-libbing of our
own in three readings.

I

Much madness is divinest sense
Much sense the starkest madness
In this, as all, prevails.
Demur, you're straightway dangerous.

II

To a discerning eye
'Tis the majority
Assent, and you are sane;
And handled with a chain.

These two versions print alternate lines without change except in the
modernization of punctuation offered by Oscar Williams in his anthology.
Here is the original in Johnson.

Much Madness is divinest Sense—
To a discerning Eye—
Much Sense—the starkest Madness—
'Tis the Majority
In this, as All, prevail—

> Assent—and you are sane—
> Demur—you're straightway dangerous—
> And handled with a Chain—

Having experimented sufficiently, I can testify that this sort of thing can be done with a large number of poems with not more damage than in the present instance; and I chose this one only because it is short and would not clutter the page. If the reader turns to "I cannot live with you" (#640), he will see what fun he can have; and see also how manners and style can make a breach in moral sentiments—but if that statement seems too formal, I will merely say that these provisional re-arrangements (otherwise quite without tampering), represent something interesting about the structure both of Emily Dickinson's mind and of her verse: a cruel freedom which will not itself be tampered with; also that it represents something profound about the deeper forms of her notation, both in verse and in the movements of her psyche. It is the sort of thing that happens to poetry when it is released from the patterning barriers of syntax and the force of residual reason.

To say this is not to attack, or to diminish the value or the force of the poetry; but merely to indicate that in the dates of her life if not in her deliberate theoretic practice she was sympathetic to kinds of poetry she probably never heard of and would have repudiated morally, if not aesthetically, if she had heard of them. This is the chain of poetry which runs from Baudelaire through surrealism and, if you like, into existentialism. I look to the new French, at the next outbreak of war, to see this in Emily Dickinson, so that they may create out of her a new theory of correspondence, a new, complex, and non-architectural syntax (for by then we shall dislike like the imposition of death the modern architecture and the faded modern abstractionism) much as some of their immediate ancestors saw or felt incentive in Poe with less cause. In the meantime, I refer the reader, both of this review and of Mr. Johnson's excellent edition of Emily Dickinson, to Marcel Raymond's *From Baudelaire to Surrealism* (New York: George Wittenborn, Inc., 1949) as a means of establishing her as a member in good standing of the intellectual movement of modern poetry. Poetry in this time, says he, "tended to become an ethic or some sort of irregular instrument of metaphysical knowledge"; and it is upon this sentiment that I think the business of the reading edition and the criticism of Emily Dickinson might well proceed. It would bring her nearer our own quick, and nearer, too, to the curse of our own spontaneity.

Emily Dickinson: A Poet Restored

by John Crowe Ransom

We would have to go a good way back into the present century to find the peak of that furious energy which produced our biggest and most whirling flood of verse in this country. So it is not too foolhardy to make a proposal to the literary historian: Will he not see if the principal literary event of these last twenty years or so has not been the restoration just now of an old poet? Emily Dickinson's life was spanned by the years 1830-86, and in most ways she was surely not one of our "moderns."

But I will anticipate the historian's reservation. There is one kind of literary event which we think of as primary, and it occurs when a new poet comes decisively into his powers and starts upon his unique career. But often this event occurs obscurely, and receives only a small public notice. I am sure I do not know if a poet of Emily Dickinson's stature has launched himself in these late years, as she did about a century ago. Evidently it may be much later before the full notice is ready to be taken, and when this happens it will seem only a secondary event, to that romantic conviction in us which would rate importances intrinsically and instantly, as do the judgments of Heaven. Nevertheless it is a first-rate event for our practical or civic way of thinking.

In the autumn of 1955 appeared *The Poems of Emily Dickinson,* a complete variorum edition in three volumes, in which are arranged according to a rough but ingenious chronology all the poems which survived her, reaching to a number of 1,775 precisely. The editor was Thomas H. Johnson, and the Harvard University Press, acting through its new subsidiary the Belknap Press, was the publisher. The event is having its proper effect at once; already obsolete are all those scattered books which appeared one by one in the fifty or more years following the poet's death, and gave us the only version of the poems which we could have.

This was a poet who in her whole lifetime saw only seven of her poems in print, and wanted to see no more; so graceless was the editorial touch which altered her originals. After her death the manuscripts fell into various hands, and their possession was contested; the public critic was very bold if he cared to offer much comment on the published verse when he could not know if the lines as they were printed were the lines as they had been written. The scandal lasted too long even for a community of untidy literary habits. But now it is as if suddenly, say about ten years ago, there had arisen a shamed sense of literary honor, of an obligation overdue to the public domain; and with it a burst of philanthropic action all round. The Dickinson Collection is now housed forever in Harvard's library, and Mr. Johnson was ready at the earliest possible moment to go to work on it, along with a troop of willing helpers. The Collection is complete except for one considerable set of manuscripts, and that too was made available for his edition.

Many editors and critics will follow up Mr. Johnson's sound labors. For example, the Dickinson reader is not going to repair to the Harvard library, nor even as a rule possess himself of Mr. Johnson's three volumes, but will require a Dickinson Anthology, or Selected Poems Edition; and he will probably get more than one. Shall we say that the poems which are destined to become a common public property might be in the proportion of one out of seventeen of the 1,775? They will hardly be more. But it will take time to tell.

And even when the poems are selected there will be hundreds of times when the editors will have to make hard decisions about straightening out some of those informalities in the manuscripts. Emily Dickinson was a little home-keeping person, and while she had a proper notion of the final destiny of her poems she was not one of those poets who had advanced to that late stage of operations where manuscripts are prepared for the printer, and the poet's diction has to make concessions to the publisher's style-book. She never found reason to abandon her habit of capitalizing her key-words, but her editor will have to reckon with certain conventions. He will respect those capitalizations, I think, even while he is removing them. They are honorable, and in their intention they are professional, and even the poet who does not practice them must have wanted to; as a way of conferring dignity upon his poetic objects, or as a mythopoetic device, to push them a little further into the fertile domain of myth. The editor will also feel obliged to substitute some degree of formal punctuation for the cryptic dashes which are sprinkled over the poet's lines; but again reluctantly, because he will know that the poet expected the sharp phrases to fall into their logical places for any reader who might be really capable of the quick intuitional processes of verse.

Since I have intimated so strong a sense of the event, I must not wait a moment longer to exhibit some of the characteristic poems, in order that my reader and I may have exactly the same poet before us. I give the poems not quite as they were written, but altered with all possible forbearance. For in none of the poems in its manuscript form has there been so much as a single line wasted on a title, and I shall identify ours by the serial numbers and the dates which Mr. Johnson has assigned to them.

And since this was a strange poet, I shall begin with two of the stranger poems; they deal with Death, but they are not from the elegiac poems about suffering the death of others, they are previsions of her own death. In neither does Death present himself as absolute in some brutal majesty, nor in the role of God's dreadful minister. The transaction is homely and easy, for the poet has complete sophistication in these matters, having attended upon deathbeds, and knowing that the terror of the event is mostly for the observers. In the first poem a sort of comic or Gothic relief interposes, by one of those homely inconsequences which may be observed in fact to attend even upon desperate human occasions.

465 (1862)

I heard a fly buzz when I died.
The stillness in the room
Was like the stillness in the air
Between the heaves of storm.

The eyes around had rung them dry,
And breaths were gathering firm
For that last onset when the King
Be witnessed in the room.

I willed my keepsakes, signed away
What portion of me be
Assignable, and then it was
There interposed a fly,

With blue, uncertain, stumbling buzz
Between the light and me;
And then the windows failed, and then
I could not see to see.

The other poem is a more imaginative creation. It is a single sustained metaphor, all of it analogue or "vehicle" as we call it nowadays, though the character called Death in the vehicle would have borne the same name in the real situation or "tenor." Death's victim now is the shy spinster, so he presents himself as a decent civil functionary making a call upon a lady to take her for a drive.

712 (1863)

Because I could not stop for Death,
He kindly stopped for me;
The carriage held but just ourselves,
And Immortality.

We slowly drove, He knew no haste,
And I had put away

My labor and my leisure too,
For His civility.

We passed the school, where children strove
At recess, in the ring.
We passed the fields of gazing grain,
We passed the Setting Sun.

Or rather, He passed us;
The dews drew quivering and chill,
For only gossamer my gown,
My tippet only tulle.

We paused before a House that seemed
A swelling of the ground;
The roof was scarcely visible,
The cornice in the ground.

Since then 'tis centuries, and yet
Feels shorter than the day
I first surmised the horses' heads
Were toward Eternity.

Next, two little extravagances or fantasies. The first is like a Mother Goose rhyme, with a riddle which it takes a moment to interpret:

1032 (1865)

Who is the East?
The Yellow Man
Who may be Purple if he can
That carries in the Sun.

Who is the West?
The Purple Man
Who may be Yellow if he can
That lets Him out again.

The other exhibits an action such as would be commonplace for the Portrait of the Artist as a Kind Maternal Woman, but that the setting could only have existed in her exotic imagination:

566 (1862)

A Dying Tiger moaned for drink;
I hunted all the sand,
I caught the dripping of a rock
And bore it in my hand.

His mighty balls in death were thick,
But searching I could see
A vision on the retina
Of water, and of me.

'Twas not my blame, who sped too slow;
'Twas not his blame, who died
While I was reaching him; but 'twas—
The fact that he was dead.

The concluding line is flat, like some ironic line by Hardy. Its blankness
cancels out the expostulation we had expected, and pure contingency
replaces the vicious agent we would have blamed, and there is nothing
rational to be said. Who is going to blame a fact?

And of course there must be some poems about nature. It is still true
that the spontaneous expression of our metaphysical moods—that consciousness whose objects are emphatically *not* those given to the senses—
is to be found in the incessant and spacious drama of the natural world.
Poets are much more concerned with earth than with Heaven. And why
not? Natural events have visibility, and audibility too; yet they seem
touched with Heavenly influences, and, if you like, they are sufficiently
mysterious. But it is common belief among readers (among men readers
at least) that the woman poet as a type is only too familiar with this
philosophy, and makes flights into nature rather too easily and upon
errands which do not have metaphysical importance enough to justify so
radical a strategy. And they might want to cite many poems by Emily
Dickinson, concerning her bees and butterflies perhaps. But see the following:

1084   (1866)

At half past three, a single bird
Unto a silent sky
Propounded but a single term
Of cautious melody.

At half past four, experiment
Had subjugated test,
And lo, Her silver Principle
Supplanted all the rest.

At half past seven, Element
Nor implement was seen,
And Place was where the Presence was,
Circumference between.

The times are half past three and half past four in the morning and half past seven in the evening of a summer's day. Where has the music gone, the silver Principle, when it grows dark? To some far corner of Circumference, the poet says, and that is a term she is fond of using. Perhaps it means: the World of all the Mysteries, where Principles have not necessarily perished when they have vanished. There is great metaphysical weight in that Circumference—as there is in Principle and Element, or in Immortality and Eternity in the second Death poem above. I suggest that there is a special Americanism here. It has been remarked how much of our political feeling has turned on abstract key-words like Democracy and Equality and Federal Principle and Constitution, and even now perhaps turns on new ones like United Nations and Conference at the Summit. These are resonant words, and the clang of them is Latinical and stylistically exact yet provocative. Our poet had a feeling for the metaphysical associations of her Latinities, and almost always invoked them when she dealt with ultimate or theological topics: the topics of the Soul. But here is a small nature poem which is of a more conventional order:

757　(1863)

The Mountains grow unnoticed;
Their purple figures rise
Without attempt, Exhaustion,
Assistance, or Applause.

In Their Eternal Faces
The Sun with just delight
Looks along, and last, and golden,
For fellowship at night.

(*Further Poems of Emily Dickinson*. Copyright 1929 by Martha Dickinson Bianchi.)

And finally, a group of personal poems. These will be from the large category of Emily Dickinson's love poems. They begin in 1861, when the poet has turned thirty, and now she professes experiences which become decisive upon the direction of her poetry. These crucial poems often have an erotic tone which is unmistakable. The dates assigned to these as to all poems are based on the handwriting, which changes perceptibly from one period to another. It changed most of all in 1861. The strokes became bold and long and uneven, tending toward the separation of the characters, and registering, for Mr. Johnson's expert staff, strong emotional disturbance. The boldness persisted into other years, of course, but the unevenness subsided, as if to witness a gradually achieved serenity. The first of our poems testifies to a mutual flame that has been fully acknowledged and enacted, and this is the time of that despair which comes after its denial.

293 (1861)

I got so I could hear his name
Without—tremendous gain—
That stop-sensation on my Soul,
And thunder in the room.

I got so I could walk across
That angle in the floor,
Where he turned so, and I turned how,
And all our sinew tore.

I got so I could stir the box
In which his letters grew,
Without that forcing, in my breath,
As staples driven through;

Could dimly recollect a Grace
(I think they call it "God")
Renowned to ease extremity,
When formula had failed;

And shape my hands, petition's way,
Tho' ignorant of a word
That Ordination utters;
My business with the Cloud;

If any Power behind it be
Not subject to Despair,
It cares in some remoter way
For so minute affair
As Misery—: Itself too great
For interrupting more.

(*Further Poems of Emily Dickinson.* Copyright 1929 by Martha Dickinson Bianchi.)

And the next poem is dated in the following year, and continues a little more resignedly in that same stage after first love when it is enough to receive new letters from the beloved.

636 (1862)

The way I read a letter's this:
'Tis first I lock the door,
And push it with my fingers next,
My transport to make sure;

And then I go the furthest off
To counteract a knock,

> Then draw my little letter forth
> And slowly pick the lock;
>
> Then glancing narrow at the wall,
> And narrow at the floor
> For firm conviction of a mouse
> Not exorcised before,
>
> Peruse how infinite I am
> To no one that you know,
> And sigh for lack of Heaven, but not
> The Heaven God bestow.

But now we come to the famous poem which displays the image of the Soul electing her lover to be now her one "Society," her communing Fellow Soul even though physically absent. Renunciation has succeeded upon Despair; it has its own happiness and even an arrogance befitting a Soul assured by Heaven.

> 303 (1862)
>
> The Soul selects her own Society,
> Then shuts the Door;
> To her divine Majority
> Present no more.
>
> Unmoved she notes the Chariots pausing
> At her low gate;
> Unmoved though Emperor be kneeling
> Upon her Mat.
>
> I've known her from an ample nation
> Choose One,
> Then close the valves of her attention
> Like Stone.

Our final poem stands only three poems later than this, in Mr. Johnson's arrangement. If that is approximately correct, the speaker has learned her lesson fast, almost too fast for the human drama becoming to her situation. She is talking now about those Superior Instants when the Soul's Society is God, and all that is of earth, including the beloved, is withdrawn. This is a Platonic or a Christian climax, and the last fruits of renunciation. I cannot think it represents a moment quite characteristic of this poet, or of poets generically. She indicates in many poems her acceptance of the saying that in Heaven there is no marrying nor giving in marriage. But the Colossal Substance of existence there is made magnificent by the flood of Latinities, which appear to render their objects with technical precision, and yet really point to objects that are ineffable.

306 (but undated)

The Soul's Superior instants
Occur to Her alone,
When friend and earth's occasion
Have infinite withdrawn,

Or She Herself ascended
To too remote a Height
For lower recognition
Than Her Omnipotent.

This Mortal Abolition
Is seldom, but as fair
As Apparition, subject
To Autocratic Air;

Eternity's disclosure
To favorites, a few,
Of the Colossal Substance
Of Immortality.

(The Single Hound. Copyright 1914 by Martha Dickinson Bianchi.)

Emily Dickinson is one of those poets who make almost constant use of the first person singular. If the poems are not autobiographical in the usual sense of following actual experience—and it is not likely that they do, inasmuch as the poetic imagination is scarcely going to consent to be held captive to historical fact, and prevented from its own free flight—then they are autobiographical in the special sense of being true to an imagined experience, and that will be according to the dominant or total image which the artist proposes to make up for herself. I suppose it is the common understanding that a poem records an experience which is at least possible, and we enter into it, by and large, because it is better than our actual experience; it does us good, and it gratifies those extravagant aspirations which we cherish secretly though proudly for ourselves. And as Emily Dickinson went from poem to poem, I must suppose that she was systematically adapting her own experience, which by common standards was a humdrum affair of little distinction, into the magnificent image of her Soul which she has created in the poems. It may have been imaginary in the first instance, but it becomes more and more actual as she finds the courage to live by it.

There was another public event associated with the definitive edition: in the appearance of *Emily Dickinson; An Interpretive Biography,* written by Mr. Johnson himself, and published at the same time as the poems and by the same house. I have a good deal of confidence in Mr. Johnson's setting out of both the primary or original image of Emily Dickinson as an actual person and the later and greater image of her literary personality. It is a good book, though far too short and lacking in documentation to be a definitive one; sometimes Mr. Johnson tells his findings without taking his readers into his confidence by showing them his evidences. But as compared with earlier biographers he is superior indeed.

It is the love poems which are decisive for the literary personality of Emily Dickinson. Most probably the poems would not have amounted to much if the author had not finally had her own romance, enabling her to fulfill herself like any other woman. She always had quick and warm affections for people, and she loved nature spontaneously with what Wordsworth might almost have called a passion. But here are the love poems, with their erotic strain. Now it happens that the god was in this instance again a blind god, or perhaps we should allow also for the possibility that the style of the romance fitted exactly into a secret intention of her own—at any rate it still appears to be the fact, for Mr. Johnson confirms it, that her grand attachment was directed to the person of a blameless clergyman who was already married. She could never have him. We know next to nothing as to what passed between them, for his letters to her have all been destroyed, except apparently for one letter, pastoral but friendly in its tone. And what becomes of the experience asserted so decently yet passionately in the poems? That was all imaginary, says Mr. Johnson roundly, if I follow him; and does not even add that it was necessary to the effectiveness of the poems. It would seem very likely that he is right about the fact; it is so much "in character," insofar as we are able to understand herself and her situation. Mr. Johnson is himself a native and a historian of her region, the valley of the Connecticut at Amherst, where in her time the life and the metaphysics were still in the old Puritan tradition, being almost boastfully remote from what went on across the state in Boston. In her Protestant community the gentle spinsters had their assured and useful place in the family circle, they had what was virtually a vocation. In a Roman community they might have taken the veil. But Emily Dickinson elected a third vocation, which was the vocation of poet. And the point is that we cannot say she deviated in life from her honest status of spinster, and did not remain true to the vows of this estate, so to speak, as did the innumerable company of her sisters. But it was otherwise for the literary personality which she now projected.

We can put this most topically nowadays, perhaps, if we say that about 1861, when Emily Dickinson had come into her thirties, she assumed in all seriousness her vocation of poet and therefore, and also, what William Butler Yeats would have called her poet's mask: the personality which was antithetical to her natural character and identical with her desire. By nature gentle but indecisive, plain in looks, almost anonymous in her want of any memorable history, she chose as an artist to claim a heroic history which exhibited first a great passion, then renunciation and honor, and a passage into the high experiences of a purified Soul. That is the way it would seem to figure out. And we have an interesting literary parallel if we think in these terms about the poetry of her contemporary, Walt Whitman. A good deal of notice has been paid lately to Whitman by way of pointing out that he was an impostor, because the aggressive masculinity which he asserted so blatantly in the poems was only assumed. But that would be Walt Whitman's mask. Whitman and Emily Dickinson were surely the greatest forces of American poetry in the nineteenth century, and both had found their proper masks. (Poe would be the third force, I think; just as original, but not a poetic force that was at the same time a moral force.)

But in Emily Dickinson's own time and place she could not but be regarded as an unusually ineffective instance of the weaker sex. She was a spinster, becoming more and more confirmed in that character. And not a useful spinster, but a recluse, refusing to enter into the world. Next, an eccentric; keeping to her room, absenting herself even from household and kitchen affairs. Perhaps a sort of poet, but what of that? The town of Amherst knew she could make verses for Saint Valentine's Day, and was always ready to send somebody a poem to accompany a flower, or a poem to turn a compliment or a condolence; once in a long while it was known that a poem got into print; but it scarcely mattered. It is a great joke now, though not at her expense, to discover with Mr. Johnson that the poems sent out on these occasions were often from her very finest store.

The slighting of the professional poet in her life-time is made up for in our time by especial gallantries on her behalf and an exquisite hatred for those who neglected her. Perhaps the most satisfying image of her, from this perspective, would now see Emily Dickinson as a kind of Cinderella, in a variant version of the story with a different moral. The original story surely sprang from man's complacent image of woman. The Ur-Cinderella scrubbed away at her pots and pans and never stopped until the kind Prince came by and took her away to his palace, where virtue had its reward. Our own Cinderella could do without the Prince; she preferred her clergyman, and he did not take her anywhere. She proceeded to take her own self upstairs, where she lived, happy ever after with her memories, her images, and her metaphysics.

She busied herself with writing, revising, and sometimes fabulously perfecting those slight but intense pieces; for the eye of the future. When there were enough of them she would stitch them down the sides together into a packet, like a little book, and put it into the cherry bureau drawer. We may suppose that she did not fail to wonder sometimes, in that ironical wisdom which steadied and protected her: What if her little packets might never catch the great public eye? But this was not her responsibility.

Among her most literate acquaintances it is scarcely possible that there was one (or more than one, says Mr. Johnson) who would not have told her, had it not been too cruel, that if she was clever enough to know the accomplishments it took to make a real poet, she would be clever enough to know better than try to be one. Consider her disabilities. She had a good school education which gave her some Latin, but after a year in Miss Lyon's advanced school for young ladies at Mount Holyoke she did not return, and we cannot quite resolve the ambiguity of whether this was due to her wish or to her poor health. She read well but not widely; the literature which gave her most was the hymnbook. And she was amazed when she was asked why she did not travel; was there not enough of the world where she was already? When she made her decision to be a poet, it is true that she sent some poems to a man of letters, and wanted to know if she should continue. The gentleman answered kindly, and entered into a lifelong correspondence with her, but did not fail to put matters on a proper footing by giving her early to understand that she might as well not seek to publish her verse. And she made little effort to find another counsellor. Perhaps it seemed to her that there was no particular correlation between being a poet and having the literary companionship of one's peers.

Of course all her disabilities worked to her advantage. Let us have a look at that hymnbook. She had at hand, to be specific, a household book which was well known in her period and culture, Watts' *Christian Psalmody*. (Her father's copy is still to be seen.) In it are named, and illustrated with the musical notations, the Common Meter, the Long, the Short, and a dozen variations which had been meticulously carried out in the church music of her New England. Her own poems used these forms with great accuracy, unless sometimes she chose to set up variations of her own, or to relax and loosen the rules. Since she was perfect in her command of these meters, they gave her a formal mastery over the substantive passions of the verse. But since these meters excluded all others, their effect was limiting. Her meters are all based upon Folk Line, the popular form of verse, and the oldest in our language. I have been used to saying that the great classics of this meter are the English Ballads and Mother Goose, both very fine, and certainly finer than most of the derivative verse done by our poets since the middle of the eighteenth century. Hereafter I must remember to add another to these classics: the Protestant hymnbooks, but especially the poetry of Emily Dickinson, which is their derivative. Folk Line is disadvantageous if it is used on the wrong poetic occasion, or if it denies to the poet the use of English Pentameter when that would be more suitable. Pentameter is the staple of what we may call the studied or "university" poetry, and it is capable of containing and formalizing many kinds of substantive content which would be too complex for Folk Line. Emily Dickinson appears never to have tried it.

The final disability which I have to mention, and which for me is the most moving, has been most emphatically confirmed in Mr. Johnson's book. Her sensibility was so acute that it made her excessively vulnerable to personal contacts. Intense feeling would rush out as soon as sensibility apprehended the object, and flood her consciousness to the point of helplessness. When visitors called upon the family, she might address them from an inner door and then hide herself; but if deep affection was involved she was likely to send word that she must be excused altogether, and post a charming note of apology later. She kept up her relations with many friends, but they were conducted more and more by correspondence; and in that informal genre she was of the best performers of the century. The happy encounter was as painful as the grievous one. But we need not distress ourselves too sorely over this disability when we observe the sequel. It made her practice a kind of art on all the social occasions; conducting herself beautifully though rather theatrically in the oral exchanges, and writing her notes in language styled and rhythmed remarkably like her poetry.

It was even better than that. The poet's Soul, she might have said, must have its housekeeping, its economy, and that must be severe in proportion as the profuse sensibility, which is the poet's primary gift, tends to dissipate and paralyze its force; till nothing remains but a kind of exclamatory gaping. The Soul must learn frugality, that is, how to do with a little of the world, and make the most of it; how to concentrate, and focus, and come remorseless and speedy to the point. That is a kind of renunciation; all good poets are familiar with it. And critics, too, I believe. Do we not all profess a faith in the kind of art which looks coolly upon the turgid deliverance of sensibility and disciplines it into beauty?

Emily Dickinson

by Austin Warren

Thomas Johnson has produced what has long been desired—a carefully edited and annotated *complete* text of Emily Dickinson's poems.[1]

It fills three large volumes. The format seems, and is, incongruous with the nature of Emily's poems, so characteristically and richly short—and, as Johnson remarks, always in revision shortened, not lengthened.

This is not the edition in which to enjoy Emily. I recall the pleasure of reading her in the slender gray volumes of the 1890's. For pleasure, as for edification, Emily should not be read in big tomes, or much of her at a time. Johnson prints 1775 poems. I felt the immediate need to reduce them to three hundred or less. Many of her poems are exercises, or autobiographical notes, or letters in verse, or occasional verses. There are poems which are coy or cute; others which are romantically melodramatic.

But the business of the scholar is to publish all the "literary remains," to establish a correct text, to elucidate obscure words or references,—whenever possible, by the citation of apposite passages from his writer's other poems or prose (in Emily's case, there are her own brilliant letters); to make possible the study of a poet's development by fixing, with what precision may be possible, the dates of composition.

These tasks of an editor Johnson has carefully and satisfactorily fulfilled. To do them, it was necessary to have access to Emily Dickinson's original manuscripts,—her penciled jottings, her worksheets and the little stitched books or "packets" into which at intervals she collected her final or semi-final versions. These "packet" versions provide—when, as for the vast majority of the poems, they are available—the authoritative text, that of the author's most considered judgment.

In the past, Emily Dickinson suffered from two sets of editors. Mrs. Todd could decipher Emily's handwriting; but she and Colonel Higginson, the minor poet and man of letters who became Emily's half-reluctant

"Emily Dickinson," From *The Sewanee Review* (Autumn 1957). Copyright © 1957 by The University of the South. Reprinted by permission of the author and *The Sewanee Review*.

[1] Thomas H. Johnson, ed., *The Poems of Emly Dickinson, Including variant readings critically compared with all known manuscripts* (Cambridge: The Belknap Press of Harvard University Press, 1955). 3 vols.

mentor, felt the need to amend so far as they could Emily's deviations
from normal educated usage—her provincial words, her use of the subjunctive in subordinate clauses, her "inaccurate" rhymes. Emily's niece,
Mme. Bianchi, less skilled at the handwriting, latterly difficult, was given
to exploiting her aunt's strangeness. It used to be thought that Mme.
Bianchi, who so shrewdly "discovered" further poems at marketable sea-
son, perhaps constructed some of the weaker ones; but this conjecture is
tacitly refuted by a study of the originals.

In "Notes on the Present Text," Johnson exhibits his fidelity to Emily's
spelling (some of it, like "Febuary," is notation of rural New England
speech habits), her capitalization, and her punctuation. The latter are
capricious. She inclines to capitalize nouns (after the fashion of Carlyle
and the German language); her capitalization of adjectives cannot be
reduced to principle. The dash is almost her exclusive mark of punctuation, exceeding much the latitude allowed to nineteenth century women.
It sometimes stands for the comma, sometimes indicates the pause of
anticipation or suspense, sometimes might be described as equivalent to
the phrasing marks of music. But categories do not suffice. Take no. 344,
for example:

> Twas the old—road—through pain—
> That unfrequented—one—
> With many a turn—and thorn—
> That stops—at heaven—
>
> This—was the Town—she passed—
> There—where she—rested—last—
> Then—stepped more fast—
> The little tracks—close pressed.

The dashes before "through pain," "and thorn," "at heaven," and
"last" mark the pauses of suspense and anticipation. Those separating off
"That unfrequented one," an appositive, might, in current use, be commas or dashes. Those at the ends of lines 5 and 6 stand for commas or
semicolons. But what of the dashes separating "old" and "road," or "unfrequented" and "one," or "This" and "was," "There" and "where"?
These seem designed to phrase: in the first two instances, indicating stress
on both the adjective and the noun, in the last two, giving the stress of
italics to "This" and "There"; probably the enclosure of "rested" is also
to ensure its being stressed. The dash in the eighth line seems intended to
emphasize the seeming contradiction between "little" and "close pressed."

I analyze this specimen to show both the oddity of Emily's pointing
and also the difficulty of repunctuating it in any fashion which does not
constitute an interpretation. Johnson says, "Quite properly such 'punctuation' can be omitted in later editions, and the spelling and capitalization

regularized, as surely she would have expected had the poems been published in her lifetime." Editions for general reading should undoubtedly
"regularize"; but how to treat Emily's punctuation is the difficult point.
Apart from her periods, the overall effect of the dashes is either to re-
produce pauses in her own reading of the poems or to render the clauses
and phrases a fluidity of transition lost by a rigid system. The best method
I can propose is to omit—after the fashion of some contemporary poetry
—all punctuation, or all save that of the period: a method which would
not, in any case I can summon up, obscure the comprehension of her
poetry.

The poems, through no. 1648, are now presented in a chronological
arrangement—the dating based partly on allusions to contemporary
events, partly on the dates of letters in which they were enclosed, partly
on the changes in Emily's handwriting (on which an "expert" contributes
a special essay), partly on the order of the "packets" in which the final
versions were placed, from the earliest packet, assembled in 1858, to the
latest in 1872.

The packet poems constitute two-thirds of her poetry. Nos. 1649-1775
Johnson does not attempt to date. These poems, for which no autograph
copies exist, are printed from transcripts, chiefly those made by Emily's
sister-in-law. Though properly put together, at the end of Vol. III, their
authenticity can scarcely be doubted. They include a few of Emily Dickinson's snake poems and "Elysium is as far as to/The very nearest Room."

Long ago I worked out my own chart of Emily's poetic development,
setting off as "early" the conventional and sentimental pieces, and using
as my tests for the mature poems the increasing substitution for rhyme of
assonance and consonance and the increasing freshness and precision of
language. I postulated a consistency of method: expected the poems systematically to grow more Dickinsonian. Having achieved her manner, her
best style, she could not, I supposed, have turned back to styles not so
definitely hers.

This theory was too neat. Emily did, to the end, "look back." Unlike
Mozart and Beethoven and Hopkins and James, she had no "late manner"
so integrally held that she could not, in conscience, deviate therefrom.

This inconsistency was certainly helped by her ambiguous character of
being a poet yet not a publishing poet. She never sharply differentiated
between poetry and occasional verse and prose. The prose of her letters
is so metonymic and metaphoric and cryptic as to be always the prose of
a poet and thus to admit the intercalation of verse written as prose.

In 1860, Emily wrote "If I shouldn't be alive/When the Robins come"
with its admirable "trying/With my granite Lip" and "How many times
these low feet staggered/Only the soldered mouth can tell"; but in the
same year she wrote the sentimental piece with its bit of Scots—probably
represented for her by Burns—"Poor little Heart!/Did they forget
thee?/Then dinna care!" and the balladic repetition of "That scalds me

now—that scalds me now" of no. 193. In 1861, she wrote "There's a certain slant of light" but also "Why—do they shut me out of heaven"—one of her "little girl" pieces. And in "about 1865" she wrote the quatrain, of which I italicize some words:

> To help our *Bleaker* parts
> *Salubrious* Hours are given
> Which if they do not fit for Earth
> *Drill Silently* for Heaven.

She had written "Arrange the heart" and rejected it for "Drill silently" —an improvement both in sparing the "heart" and in giving the double-sensed *drill* (the martial discipline; the carpenter's tool if not then the dentist's also). Yet at the same time she wrote "Let down the Bars, Oh Death," a tritely sentimental sheep-and-shepherd poem.

Emily added to her styles without subtracting; and in maturity she wrote a new kind of poetry without relinquishing the liberty of slipping back into her earlier modes.

II

It used to be said of Emerson that his "bad" rhymes were due to a deficient ear—a theory once and for all disproved by the publication, in the first volume of Rusk's *Letters,* of the earliest poems of Emerson, written in perfectly accurate heroic couplets. Even the early Whitman could rhyme and meter acceptably. And Emily's first known verses, written in the early 1850's, demonstrate likewise that her subsequent deviation was purposed. Her "Valentine" poem faithfully rhymes "swain" and "twain," "air" and "fair." But, having said that, I have to add that none of them would have become known as poets for these "correct" productions. By intuition, and by relatively conscious theorizing, they had to create new kinds of poetry.

Like Whitman, Emily took off from Emerson, whose *Poems* and *Essays* she owned and knew; but Whitman took off from Emerson's theory of the poet and his poetic and rhetorical essays; Emily, from Emerson's own practice as a poet: his short-lined rhyming; his gnomic quatrains and gnomic short poems like "Brahma"; his "Hamatreya."

This lineage from Emerson was blended with another lineage—that of the hymnal. Several times she quotes Isaac Watts' hymn beginning, "There is a land of pure delight":

> Could we but climb where Moses stood
> And view the landscape o'er,
> Nor Jordan's stream, nor death's cold flood
> Should fright us from the shore;

and the stanza, with its alternating 4 and 3, remains one of her metrical favorites. She creates a counterpoint or descant on Watts, relaxing the rhyming of lines 1 and 3 and the personalizing of Watts' congregational pieces:

> 'Tis not that Dying hurts us so—
> 'Tis living—hurts us more—
> But Dying is a different way—
> A Kind behind the Door . . .

Short meter, long meter, common meter—the standard hymn stanzas—are her mold, not to break but to render pliant.

Emily's language is her own mixture of provincialisms, standard speech of her time, the concrete and the abstract, the words of young people and the theological words of orthodox preachers (e.g., infinite). Her use of language is almost unfailingly meditated and precise. Worksheet drafts for a few of her poems provide the list of alternatives from which she chose. In the poem on the Bible (no. 1545), the epithet finally elected—"warbling"—was chosen out of these possible dissyllables: "typic, hearty, bonnie, breathless, spacious, tropic, warbling, winning, mellow." None of these dissyllables seems inevitable; but warbling—the unpremeditated singing of a bird or a rustic—seems the best candidate. Of a clergyman ("He preached upon 'Breadth' till it argued him narrow") she asserts satirically that Jesus would not know how to "meet so *enabled* a man," choosing her epithet from "learned, religious, accomplished, discerning, accoutred, established, conclusive." Emily needs a trisyllabic word: but she certainly also distinguished it from "able": to "enable" is legally, as by authority, to make one what, by nature, he is *not*: it suggests the pretentiousness of borrowed righteousness or of learning extraneous to the personality.

Previous editions have printed the last stanza of "I never saw a Moor" as

> I never spoke with God
> Nor visited in heaven—
> Yet certain am I of the spot
> As if the chart were given.

Johnson reads, for the conventional "chart," the word "checks," in the colloquial sense of railroad tickets, quoting in adequate support Emily's prose, "My assurance of existence of Heaven is as great as though, having surrendered my checks to the conductor, I knew that I had arrived there." In no. 391, "A Visitor in Marl," Mme. Bianchi's *Unpublished Poems* reads "March" for "Marl." Neither here nor when, in a note, he cites Emily's writing of her dead father as "lying in Marl," does Johnson gloss this unusual but accurate word. The "Visitor" is Death; and the word "Marl" means an earthy, crumbling deposit chiefly of clay, mixed with calcium carbonate, or earth (in the sense of clay): it means the cadaver. These two examples will illustrate that Emily used the words she meant, and the gain of their restoration.

III

As Allen Tate long ago remarked, Emily stands, among New Englanders, between Emerson and Hawthorne,—of whom she wrote that he "entices—appalls." Her rearing was in Trinitarian Congregationalism—often in New England villages referred to as—in contrast to Unitarian heresy—the Orthodox Church. Unlike the rest of her family (some of whom capitulated early, some later), Emily never "joined the church," never would fix the content of her belief; but she knew what her neighbors and her pastor believed, and—like Emerson in his attacks on Harvard College—had the personal comfort and poetic license of cherishing favorite scepticisms without supposing that they would undermine, and hence render impossible of attack, the solid faith of others, the solid force of institutions. She lacks Hawthorne's sense of sin, and isolation for privacy is hardly an evil to her; the analogy to Hawthorne lies rather in her obsession with death and futurity,—still more the sense of mystery: as in the remark (put on the lips of Holgrave), "I begin to suspect that a man's bewilderment is the measure of his wisdom." Her deepest poems are metaphysical or tragic; her mode of vision symbolist—thinking in analogies. Emerson (whose *Essays* an early "tutor" gave her) may have flexed her mind, encouraged her speculations and her questionings of orthodoxy; but her mythology remains—what Hawthorne's was and Emerson's never—Biblical and Trinitarian. She is a rebel—but not, like Emerson, a schismatic.

A third ancestor comes often to my mind,—Sir Thomas Browne, a writer dear to the 19th century New Englanders, especially to the Concord men, and known and cited by Emily. "For prose," she wrote Colonel Higginson, she had "Mr. Ruskin, Sir Thomas Browne, and the *Revelations*." These are very special kinds of prose certainly; and I don't hesitate to say that Emily's poetic style is not only that of some Emerson poems ("The Humble Bee," "Hamatreya," "Mithridates," "Days") but that of Browne's *Religio* and *Christian Morals*. Her world view is the Brunonian sense of the natural world, so full of curious objects in the eyes of most men—though, as Browne remarks, he doesn't know how we can call the toad ugly when it was made by the express design of God to assume that shape. Nor is Emily going to simplify the complexity of a God who made the bat. Of the bat, Emily writes (1575):

> Deputed from what Firmament—
> Of what Astute Abode—

> Empowered with what Malignity
> Auspiciously withheld—
> To his adroit Creator
> Ascribe no less the praise—
> Beneficent, believe me,
> His Eccentricities.

Browne heaps up technical difficulties which beset the acceptance of the Bible and orthodox theology: he delights to list such difficulties as occasioned Bishop Colenso (of Arnoldian memory) the loss of his faith—the statistics of an Ark capable of holding all the creatures said to have entered.

Emily's most characteristic difficulties are with the morals of the Bible, especially of the Old Testament,—which in her time and place had not been subjected to the "Higher Criticism." She "knew her Bible" well, the total Bible: it was her prime mythology. She neither rejects nor accepts it without question and reservation. Its histories are rich and plausible human documents; its doctrinal books, like St. Paul's epistles, are testimonials for consideration, propose questions and speculations for her theological sensibility to ponder. She would have been shocked equally by having the Bible treated as negligible, or even as "literature," or by accepting it as an infallible silencer of speculation.

Her famous "The Bible is an antique volume" was originally written for her nephew Ned and given the title, "Diagnosis of the Bible, by a Boy"; but the boy was not alien to the woman who understood his boredom and his bafflement: the final version is hers.

> The Bible is an antique Volume—
> Written by faded Men
> At the suggestion of Holy Spectres—
> Subjects—Bethlehem—
> Eden—the ancient Homestead—
> Satan—the Brigadier—
> Judas—the Great Defrauder—
> David—the Troubadour—
> Sin—a distinguished Precipice
> Others must resist—
> Had but the tale a warbling Teller—
> All the boys would come—
> Orpheus' Sermon captivated—
> It did not condemn.

The sympathy with Satan and Judas is for rebels against laws they don't understand, or it comes from a feeling that, since sin must needs come into the world, and since the Crucifixion was foretold and necessary, we should not be too hard on the unhappy perpetrators. The mushroom is a "Judas Iscariot" to the rest of Nature. Elsewhere (no. 120) she remarks that there are shocking instances of God's injustice: "Moses wasn't fairly used; Ananias wasn't." But it's temerarious to make such protestations. The same God who made the Lamb made the Lion: He who provided good and suffers the little ones to come unto Him also permits sin and evil—that "where Sin abounded, Grace may much more abound."

There have been times in which the pious felt the need to defend God to prop Him up,—as though it were our business to support the Rock and Word and Comforter. Emily is too orthodox—i.e., too inclusive—to forget that behind God the Son, Himself sturdy, is God the Father, the Creator of all things and the Abyss of Godhead, unexhausted by what His creatures understand of His ways: moving in a mysterious way His wonders to perform, and best known not defining Him.

Yet in allowing for God's ways not being our ways we mustn't use language equivocally but apply our humanly highest standards. Writing on Abraham, Isaac, and God (no. 1317), Emily doesn't hesitate to identify God with "tyranny" and to find the moral of the averted human sacrifice in the reflection that, even with a "Mastiff," "Manners may prevail." The existence of a God Emily never doubts. The "fop, the Carp, the Atheist" value the present moment, yet "their commuted feet/The Torrents of Eternity/Do all but inundate."

The problem of Belief is ever with her.

> The abdication of Belief
> Makes the Behavior small—
> Better an ignis fatuus
> Than no illume at all.

"Belief, it does not fit so/When altered frequently." There must be a Heaven because there certainly are saints on earth; and sanctity argues its survival. But how prove a sky to a mole? *Too much of proof affronts Belief.* The turtle won't try to demonstrate to us that he can move—but when we have turned our backs, he does. "That oblique Belief which we call conjecture"—is the attempt to guess what Heaven is like—to picture "What eye hath not seen"—what the "mansions" of Heaven look like. Emily speculates on the state of the dead: whether they know what is happening to us or are too removed; or whether, on the contrary, they are nearer to us for the absence of their bodies. But these are conjectures unanswered by Scriptures. Straight belief is uncircumstantial; content to affirm what it cannot map or delineate. And, for Emily, belief is straight.

IV

I heartily wish that conjecture about Emily's lovers might cease as unprofitable. Of course her poems are all "'fragments of a great confession": of course she wrote out of her life, her life on various levels. But books on who her "lover" was turn attention from the poems to the poet, and substitute detective work for criticism. Her readers of the 1890's did not require to know what "who" or "whos" gave her insight into love and renunciation, nor need we.

It is when the best of philosophers make blunders not inherent in their systems but extraneous to it—when Berkeley, in his neo-Platonic *Siris,* advocates the panacea of tar water,—that we legitimately seek a biographical explanation. And when a good poet writes inferior poems we are concerned with the reason for the badness, in order to leave, inviolate, the goodness of the other poems. But the "goodness" is not so to be explained.

One must distinguish biography from literary biography, distinguish between the study of the empirical person who wrote poems and that undeniable "personality" present in poems which makes them recognizable as written by the same person. What is biographically peculiar to the empirical person is not relevant to the "good poems," those intelligible to and valued by competent readers, which are elucidatory of our own experiences. To be sure, literary criticism can scarcely avoid a psychology of types—as it cannot dispense with a knowledge of the culture in which a poet was reared,—and, certainly, cannot lack a close intimacy with the state of the language from which the poet makes artfully expressive deviations. But biographical studies and culture-history—for those who practice them, ends in themselves—are to be used by a critic with caution and delicacy. Scholarship as such restricts a great poet to her own time, place, and empirical self. Criticism must delicately "clear" the poems for present use and evaluation—show what is for our time, or, more grandiosely, what is for all times.

I make these commonplaces of neoclassical and contemporary criticism, conscious that, in what immediately follows, I may seem to diverge from them. There is a "lion in the way" of contemporary readers of Emily— the lion of biography. It has proved impossible not to pursue, to an extent, the facts gathered and the speculations offered by those who have sought to attach Emily's power as a poet of love and death to some single love and renunciation.

A widely informed and sensible work is Mrs. Bingham's *Emily Dickinson's Home: Letters of Edward Dickinson and his Family, with Documentation and Comment* (New York: Harper & Row, Inc., 1955), which, as commentary, combines social history with family biography: I would commend specifically the chapters, "The New England Way," "Recreation," "Funerals and Fears," "Dickinson 'Difference.' " The daughter of Mrs. Todd, Emily's first editor, takes in her stride the loves, real or imaginary; and she cites the testimony of Emily's brother, William Austin. A year his sister's senior, Austin was a collector of paintings and enamoured of shrubs, the honorable assumptor of his father's responsibilities to college, town, and family, yet a more flexible and troubled character. Austin, to whom, while he was away from Amherst, Emily wrote copious letters, who, in manhood, lived in the house next door in troubled marriage with "Sister Sue," who was the affectionate brother, seems to me the most competent judge of his sister's personality. What was his judgment of the "lovers"? Asked, after Emily's death, the direct question, "Did she fall in love with the Rev. Mr. Wadsworth?" he thought not. He said that "at different times" Emily "had been devoted to several men." He even went so far as to maintain that she had been several times in love, in her own way. But he denied that because of her devotion to any one man she forsook all others. Emily "reached out eagerly, fervently even, toward anybody who lighted the spark . . ."

Wadsworth certainly mattered to Emily; and the time of his removal from Philadelphia to San Francisco, a distance prohibitive of prompt access to him by letter, coincides with significant alterations in her life and poetry. Yet this was a fantasy of love, constructed about a man whom she scarcely knew and who was doubtless never aware of her idealization. Her sense for what is real always won out over whatever presented attractive fantasy.

There were, I think, many loves in Emily's life, loves of varying kinds and durations. There were infatuations with Sister Sue and Kate Anthon, perhaps with Helen Hunt Jackson—loves "natural" enough and permitted by 19th century standards. There was a succession of males to whom she attached her devotion: some of them, like Gould, Humphrey, and Newton, and Colonel Higginson, her "teachers"; some more awesome characters.

Her father, Edward Dickinson, was a kind of version of God the Father; stern and implacable, yet a tower and rock of strength; mysterious in his ways, but doubtless always acting for the best; the man of moral rigidity who was none the less capable of ringing the church bell as for a fire so that his neighbors emerge from their houses to share a magnificent sunset.[2] Her feeling for her father was, I should guess, dominant. Her "poems about God," the "Papa in Heaven," are little girl compounds of pertness and humility addressed to a powerful and puzzling big man, to Admirable Omnipotence. Her figures psychically distant and impressive—Father, the Rev. Mr. Wadsworth, Mr. Bowles, the Editor of the *Springfield Republican,* were all "Fathers"; and God she made in their image and likeness.

[2] Actually, an Aurora Borealis. See Jay Leyda, *Years and Hours of Emily Dickinson* (New Haven, Yale University Press, 1960) I, 213-4, entries of September 29 and October 1. [Ed. note.]

It seems archetypally true of Emily to say that God was her Lover. The God whom she reverenced was not the Son, the "Paragon of Chivalry," like her brother Austin and indeed herself, but God the Father, the Lover at once infinitely attractive and infinitely awesome, one partly revealed by the Son and His nature, but only partly revealed; finally, the unattainable God. "He who loves God must not expect to be loved in return."

All of Emily's lovers were unattainable: either members of her family or women or married men; and they were doubtless loved, in her way, precisely because they were unattainable,—did not, could not, expose, even to herself, the nature of her dedication.

Emily's life is no riddle. New England had—and has—many maiden ladies like her, and many widows who are like maiden ladies. There are many who have loved unsuccessfully or insuitably—whom fear or pride have kept from the married state; many who have loved "above them," could love in no other way, and who prefer singleness to some democratic union. The father who prefers his daughters not to marry, who needs them at home with him, is matched by the daughter so filial as to prefer the tried arrangement. There is nothing monstrous—or even necessarily thwarted or blighted—about such women. They have their friends and their duties; they can nurture their own sensibilities and spiritualities—grow sharper in consciousness for their economy.

Many gradually withdraw from the world as Emily did. The circumference shrinks as friends die or depart; the pattern of life becomes more rigid. But the withdrawal can be gain if there is something to withdraw to. Most spinsters have, like Emily, their brand of humor, their mode of ritual—perhaps even their habitual way of dressing; but what differentiates Emily is that she had her poetry. She need not avert or circumvent woe save by the stratagem of poetry. She need not keep her grief to herself; she could give it to consciousness and to paper—could face it by naming it.

Many richnesses sustained Emily—among them her sense of "degree," of status, of family. Of "degree" she was positively and negatively aware. When she wasn't a little girl, to be fed a crumb, she was a Queen or an Empress, jewelled and triumphant on a throne. At once no man was "good enough" for her to marry, and those higher than she were so much higher as to seem out of reach or, in fantasy, grandly, by their election, to lift her to equality.

She was a Dickinson, the daughter of a "Squire," whose father had been one of the founders of Amherst College, whose brother was, if epigone, the honorable successor to greatness. The bonds between her and her family were such as to sustain her pride.

She was not, however she might seem to Boston, a rural poetess or spinster, but a princess. When Colonel Higginson proposed visits to Boston, access to her intellectual and literary "peers" (Julia Ward Howe, for example, or Mrs. Sargent and her monthly convenings of paper-readers and polite disputants), Emily could not be moved from Amherst. She never came to Higginson: he, and other professed admirers, had to come to her, to her home, where she could set the tone and dictate the ritual. Emerson might leave Concord for the Saturday Club; like Thoreau, Emily stayed at home.

It has often been regretted that she did not, like Whitman, tender her poems to Emerson's sympathetic inspection rather than to Higginson's mixture of admiration and critical gentility; but Emerson, despite his elegant courtesy, his mode of listening to others, could not at once be heeded—and dismissed. Emerson was polished "granite"—a master, like Emily herself, and (unlike her chosen mentors) a master in a domain too closely impinging on her own. In reputation "above" her, she was a poet-in-verse such as he but adumbrated. He could not serve in the convenient capacity of Higginson nor incite the terror of forbidden presences.

How perceptive, how shrewd to estimate those who would serve, was this New England spinster. She seized upon what she needed, but seizure sufficed: she had no taste for neighbors.

V

After the fashion of nineteenth century anthologies like Bryant's *Family Library of Poetry and Song* and Emerson's *Parnassus*, Emily's poems were first published under the headings, "Life," "Nature," "Love," and "Time and Eternity." But these categories are far from being mutually exclusive; indeed, they cannot be separated in any good poet or verse, and are not in Emily and Emily's,—for a poet thinks analogically, thinks in terms of the interaction and interpenetration of these or any other spheres of being.

Nature, to Emily, is "Animated." She anthropomorphizes: bobolink, butterfly, rat, and the snake—no stranger to us, doubtless, than our fellows, whom, in turn, we metamorphose from the creatures. Inanimate Nature is also animate, like animal or person or ghostly presence.

> An awful Tempest mashed the air—
> The clouds were gaunt, and few
> A Black—as of a Spectre's Cloak
> Hid Heaven and Earth from view.

Even the machine—the railroad train—is Animated Nature in the poem, one of a brilliant series in which, as in the Old English Riddle Poems, the object is characterized but never named, conceptualized. Her train is a mythological beast which first, catlike, *laps* the miles and *licks* the valleys up and which ends, horselike, by *neighing* and *stopping*, "docile and omnipotent/At its own stable door."

What moves is living; but death is immobile, and so are its approximations—loss, departures, removals.

Superficially, to be sure, Emily is in the line of those village versifiers whose function was to elegize the dead in broadside or for incision on slate or marble gravestones; and many of her poems were either composed, or later made to serve, as tributes to her deceased relatives, friends, Amherst acquaintances, the distant admired (Charlotte Brontë and George Eliot). Then, too, she was reared in a period in which poets like Poe, Bryant (who celebrated death from "Thanatopsis" till his own), anthologies like Cheever's *Poets of America,* and newspaper poems, often cut out and preserved in scrapbooks, made the "topic" appear particularly suited to verse. The frequency with which mortuary accounts appeared in her newspaper, the Springfield *Republican,* prompted Emily to ask a friend in 1853: "Who writes those funny accidents, where railroads meet each other unexpectedly, and gentlemen in factories get their heads cut off quite informally?" It was Amherst custom, as it was elsewhere in New England, to visit cemeteries on Sunday afternoons. The local graveyard adjoined the Dickinson orchard on Pleasant Street; and, during her youth, funeral processions passed by the Dickinson house.

These circumstances supply a tradition and mollify, if not remove, suspicion of Emily's morbidity. But, if they elucidate, they do not explain Emily's death poems, which are unlike Poe's and unlike Bryant's.

To the most cursory scanner, Emily was "much possessed by Death." "Goings away," departures, whether to geographic distances or by felt disloyalties, spacial and psychic separations, absences from us, all disjunctions, can be felt, and were, by Emily, as deaths. In a rather usual pattern of reaction, she wrote her Death poems with a quality of magnitude almost proportioned to, for her, the unimportance of the intimated "person in mind,"—the *occasion* for a poem, not its motive or momentum.

Emily's "white election," we know, began around the year 1862. This "white election": could it not have been Emily's acceptance of Death, her suicide without suicide? What "facts" are supposed to explain the "problem of Emily" point to some one, a Person unacknowledgeable to her consciousness. Her poems suggest compelled flights from impending, threatening consciousness of that person or persons.

How angry we feel when one towards whom we had felt, or protested we did, dies on us. He or she has up and left us. Ashamed of anger towards the "loved dead"—or those loved who have separated from us, one denies the feeling. Emily's "white election" is not wholly devoid of moral blackmail, consequent guilts—rich pasture for poetry.

The poems about death are ranging in kind and tone. One says that Emily's poems about death are sometimes written from the point of view of the observer; in others, she is witnessing her own death by anticipation ("You'll be sorry when I'm dead" or "I want to die"); in others she is contemplating present destitution by loss ("My life closed twice before its close"). The poems don't have to be in the first person to be self-regarding.

> On such a night, or such a night,
> Would anybody care
> If such a little figure
> Slipped quiet from its chair—

and "Twas the old—road—through pain" and the other poems about death of a little girl seem, unavoidably, Emily in such postures, quite as much as "If I shouldn't be alive . . ."

Of all the poems about death one is temerarious in distinguishing the observed from the imagined or fictive. "Looking at Death, is Dying" (281) is a maxim to be attended—even though it occurs in a poem not about death but about loss. How can one write about death without having experienced it? For whom the bell tolls, it tolls for the onlooker and is his *memento mori*.

The dead are variously conceived of,—sometimes as in their graves, quiet despite the bustle of the day and of history ("How many times these low feet staggered," "Safe in their alabaster chambers"). "I'm sorry for the dead today," light in tone, lightly pities the sleeping farmers and their wives who "rest" while the festival of haying goes on in the village about them. In another poem, the grave is a cottage where a girl plays at "Keeping house" and prepares "marble tea." And the gravestone is a kind of death-mask for the dead beneath it: it tries to thank those who gave the robin a "memorial crumb," and tries with "granite lip."

Perhaps the most brilliant of the death-in-death poems is "A clock stopped—/Not the Mantel's," a masterpiece in the employment of a conceit coterminous with the poem—a definition once proposed for Donne's poem but more accurately applied to such of Emily's as this. Most of what is said fits approximately both sides of the equation; and that intellectual work which is the conceit serves, as we know, to distance the poem.

Like a train, a clock may be felt near to animate. In fable, a clock stops when its owner dies; at any event, it measures the clock-time by which men live. The Doctor is a "Shopman," a clock-repairer; but he cannot set the heart's pendulum to swinging again. To the dead, hours, and minutes and "Seconds," are alike now meaningless. They are meaningless compared with the "Decades"—more than the meter can justify this understatement for "centuries"—the "decades of Arrogance" which separate "Dial life" from the "Degreeless Noon" of Eternity. The "Trinket," the diminutively precious object, has gained the accrual of "awe"; and the onlooker feels the "arrogance" of the dead—their unconcern for us.

This poem appears to take the stance of the onlooker; but does it? It can well be argued that the poet imagines herself at the lofty distance of death, envisages how those others will feel as they watch and witness. In a poem like this the distinction between the imagined and the imaginer becomes impossible to fix. In Emily's poems, the referent and its metaphoric referend are often difficult to distinguish.

"There's a certain slant of light" is a poem ostensibly about winter afternoons with their "Heavenly Hurt" and their "Seal Despair"; when that winter light goes, "tis like the Distance/On the look of Death." In this poem "Death" is a metaphor for winter light and at the same time winter light is a metaphor for death: one inclines to say, preponderantly the latter. "I like a look of Agony/Because I know it's true" invokes the glazing of the eyes in death; but "Beads upon the Forehead" are invoked by "Anguish"; and the death is not the death of the dead but of the living. "A *wounded* Deer—leaps highest" in the "Extasy of *death*"; yet the next metaphors, the "*smitten* rock" and the "trampled steel" are not death but, by anthropomorphic transfer, versions of that present anguish of which mirth is the cautious "Mail."

"It can't be Dying! It's too Rouge—/The Dead shall go in White" (no. 221) is a poem ostensibly about a sunset, a traditional symbol for death; but, by the familiar figure of suggesting by denying, she has occasion to speak of a kind of death. The reference to white suggests Emily's own habitual garb from this time on. In the Orient, as she may have known, white is the color of lovers who have come through great tribulation and washed their robes (cf. no. 325; Revelation 7:14) and as the color of her "blameless mystery"—perhaps in contrast to the blame-suspect black veil of Hawthorne's clergyman. White is the color for her kind of death-in-life; and the poem seems dynamized by it, with the sunset metaphor.

Suggestion by negation is most powerfully used in "It was not Death, for I stood up," a poem about death-in-life. The state deanimizes the self.

> The Figures I have seen
> Set orderly, for Burial
> Reminded me, of mine—
>
> As if my life were shaven,
> And fitted to a frame,
> And could not breathe without a key . . .

It felt like the stopping of a clock, like frost-frozen ground (deanimizing images); but most like chaos—chaos without "even a Report of Land/ To Justify—Despair."

These poems about despair are probably the best poems Emily ever wrote; but they cannot be taken as her total "message to the world."

Reading her work does not induce despair. For herself first, and then for her readers, the very articulation of despair is effectual movement towards its dispelling. The autonomy of Nature and the "creatures" constantly arouses her fascinated apprehension of the variety and flexibility of nature. If anger and fear paralyze, "self-reliance" has its resources unessayed without the felt need:

> If your Nerve, deny you—
> Go above your Nerve—
> He can lean against the Grave,
> If he fear to swerve—
>
> 'Tis so appalling—it exhilarates—
> So over Horror, it half Captivates—
> The Soul stares after it, secure—
> To know the worst, leaves no dread more—

Then there are Emily's poems about immortality, which she both doubted and affirmed—affirmed not only on Bible testimony but from the argument that as there are saints there must be a Heaven—as there is grandeur, it cannot finally perish. These poems are variously mythic: there is no Biblical warrant for "fleshless lovers" meeting in Heaven. Whatever Emily's personal belief—centrally, a belief in belief—her after-death poems are readily translatable into other terms. As God is the resource, within or without, which transcends the resources we thought were our limits, so eternity is a name for ultimate definitions of the total personality:

> Of all the Souls that stand create—
> I have elected—One—
> When Sense from Spirit—files away—
> And Subterfuge—is done—

The final sense of Emily's total achievement is the power of poetry to register and master experience.

Introduction to
Selected Poems of Emily Dickinson

by James Reeves

. . . In a curiously uneven book[1] the American critic R. P. Blackmur writes (p. 62):

> The final skill of a poet lies in his so conducting the work he does deliberately do, that the other work—the hidden work, the inspiration, the genius—becomes increasingly available not only in new poems but in old poems re-read.

Blackmur is not here discussing Emily Dickinson, and he continues:

> The only consistent exhibition of such skill in the last century is in the second half of the career of W. B. Yeats.

He is not expressly discussing Yeats: the quotation comes from an essay on Hardy, a poet with whom Blackmur is as much out of sympathy as he is with Emily. When he comes to write of her, he cannot apply his own excellent generalization to the sum of her work. The work Emily 'did deliberately'—the bathetic, contrived verses—was precisely the journeyman, apprentice work which made 'the hidden work' possible.

It is worth considering this critic's views on Emily in some detail, because, even where wrong, they are illuminating.[2] Blackmur makes a perfunctory admission of Emily's greatness, but most of his essay is concerned to deny it. He concedes that she had 'an aptitude for language' (a critical meiosis worthy of note) but objects that she was naïve and unprofessional.

"Introduction to *Selected Poems of Emily Dickinson*." From *Selected Poems of Emily Dickinson* (New York: The Macmillan Co., 1959; London: Heinemann Educational Books, 1959). Copyright © 1959 by James Reeves. Reprinted by permission of the author, The Macmillan Co. and Heinemann Educational Books. Numbers assigned to poems in this essay correspond to those in Mr. Reeves' *Selected Poems*.

[1] R. P. Blackmur, *Language as Gesture* (New York: Harcourt, Brace & World, Inc., 1952).

[2] It should be pointed out that the essay on Emily Dickinson was first published in America in 1937, when ill-considered enthusiasm for the poet was at its height.

"Success was by accident, by the mere momentum of sensibility. . . . Most of the Dickinson poems seem to have been initially as near automatic writing as may be. The bulk remained automatic, subject to correction and multiplication of detail."

The point is, surely, that there was success—not whether it came by accident or by design. And who is to prove that the greatest poetry is not "automatic writing, subject to correction"? There is of course here a question of fundamental poetic theory, which cannot now be discussed fully. Blackmur is of the school of Eliot and Auden, both of whom have expressed themselves as opposed to the idea of inspiration in poetry. He prefers poetry which is demonstrably a wrought and contrived work of art. If a poet, like a pavement-artist, can write "All my own work" beside his productions, and add "No outside help from the Muse," the Apollonian critic is satisfied. At least he knows where he is: he can analyse, assess, compare. Emily, on the other hand, like many others from Plato onwards, undoubtedly held the Dionysian view by which "All my own work" could certainly be taken as a certificate of failure. To the Dionysian poet there is no such thing as automatic writing, success is never by accident—it is by design, not of the poet but of the source of his inspiration.

Another objection Blackmur makes against Emily is on the score of her imagery.

> The most conspicuous of all is the vocabulary of romance royalty, fairy-tale kings, queens and courts, and the general language of chivalry. Emily Dickinson was as fond as Shakespeare of words like *imperial, sovereign, dominion,* and the whole collection of terms for rank and degree. Probably she got them more from Scott and the Bible and the Hymnal than from Shakespeare. There is none of Shakespeare's specific and motivating sense of kings and princes as the focus of society, and none of his rhetoric of power; there is nothing tragic in Emily Dickinson's royal vocabulary.

One would have thought that any critic would admit a hierarchical system of social organization as permissible in a poet's world. Emily's life was contained within, but not bounded by, the parochial, theocratic society of a small New England town. From this society she withdrew.

> The show is not the show
> But they that go.
> Menagerie to me
> My neighbour be.

The life she constructed for herself within, yet apart from, that society was lived in the world of her poetry; and that world was built, like the world of the classical renaissance, on a hierarchical order, in which flowers, insects, birds, animals, inanimate nature, humanity and divinity had their appointed places. It does not matter whether the pattern of her royal hierarchy derives from the Bible, from Shakespeare, or from myth and legend. It is perfectly valid within its context. The King is usually her lost lover, husband, master; the Queen is herself. It is difficult to believe that anyone could deny the tragedy in Emily's royal vocabulary who had read *I dreaded that first robin so* (No. 54), with its poignant yet triumphant assumption of the rôle of "Queen of Calvary."

Summing up, Blackmur writes: "We have a verse in great body that is part terror, part vision, part insight and observation, which must yet mostly be construed as a kind of *vers de société* of the soul—not in form or finish but in achievement."

"Terror, vision, insight, observation"—an admirable summary of the content of much of the poetry; but what are we to make of a phrase like "*vers de société* of the soul," except that it is glib, and not even a half-truth? *Vers de société* is a form of currency passed between the members of a coherent social group; it implies a community of interest and outlook. The phrase has no relevance to the situation of Emily Dickinson. And here is this critic's final judgement:

> She was neither a professional poet nor an amateur; she was a private poet who wrote indefatigably as some women cook or knit. Her gift for words and the cultural predicament of her time drove her to poetry instead of antimacassars. Neither her personal education nor the habit of her society as she knew it ever gave her the least inkling that poetry is a rational and objective *art* and most so when the theme is self-expression. She came, as Mr. Tate says, at the right time for one kind of poetry, the poetry of sophisticated, eccentric vision. That is what makes her good—in a few poems and many passages representatively great. But she never undertook the great profession of controlling the means of objective expression. That is why the bulk of her verse is not representative but mere fragmentary indicative notation. The pity of it is that the document her whole work makes shows nothing so much as that she had the themes, the insight, the observation, and the capacity for honesty, which had she only known how —or only known why—would have made the major instead of the minor fraction of her verse genuine poetry. But her dying society had no tradition by which to teach her the one lesson she did not know by instinct.

It is of course customary in some critical schools to explain the emergence of a poet in terms of "cultural predicaments" and the like. It is more difficult to explain why mid-nineteenth century New England was not a nest of singing birds, and why many of Emily's contemporaries probably did in fact make antimacassars. Poetry may be a "rational and objective art" to R. P. Blackmur, or Pope, or Boileau, or Virgil; but it was not so to Plato, or Homer, or Shelley, or Coleridge, or Emily Dickinson. One need not quarrel with "objective," but that it is a rational art there are many who would deny. It seems to me that in the case of

Emily Dickinson it was more of a rite—a rite of propitiation towards the destructive forces of nature, death on the one hand and human sensibility on the other, performed as a relief from fear and ecstasy. The best of the poems are each the resolution of a personal problem experienced while under the possession of an abnormal state of emotion. To call the means of this resolution a "rational art" is to evade most of the disputed questions about poetic creation.

Essentially Blackmur is in agreement with Higginson as to the eccentricity and indiscipline of Emily's poetry. The charge that she was neither a professional, nor an amateur, but a private poet, if it means anything, must be taken as being in Emily's favour; but that "she wrote indefatigably as some women cook," betrays an anti-feminine irritation not uncommon in this context. Emily did also cook—very expertly, we are told, and her cooking was in part a propitiation of her father, who would eat no bread but hers, and in part a contribution to the well-being of her circle. She cooked, one might say, as some men write *vers de société*. Her poems were inspired by an altogether different allegiance. A friend who is also a literary critic has suggested, not perhaps quite seriously, that "woman poet" is a contradiction in terms; and Mrs. Aphra Behn wrote of "the man in me, the poet." But it must be insisted that "poet" also, in the true sense of the word, is a contradiction in terms. The poets may in fact have been mostly men, but men are not naturally poets. The irrational rôle of poet may fall on a woman at birth as on a man. The poetic elements in, say, *Mansfield Park* or *Wuthering Heights* are a proof of this.

There may indeed be something in the feminine habit of mind which, given the right conditions, would be especially favourable to the writing of a particular kind of poetry—though not necessarily to any kind that can be called a "rational art." Allen Tate, a critic of fine perceptions, is referring, I think, without realizing it, to the feminine habit of mind when he says:

> She could not in the proper sense think at all, and unless we prefer the feeble poetry of moral ideas that flourished in New England in the eighties, we must conclude that her intellectual deficiency contributed at least negatively to her great distinction.

What Tate means is that Emily could not rationalize in the masculine way. We are not aware of intellectual deficiency in her poems, as we are aware of poetic deficiency in Elizabeth Barrett's. The latter, educated in a strenuously male discipline, tried to reason like a man. Emily reasoned, or argued, in riddles and paradoxes:

> It might be lonelier
> Without the loneliness

and

> Water is taught by thirst

and

> The thought is quiet as a flake,
> A crash without a sound,
> How life's reverberation
> Its explanation found.

It is impossible to regard such lines as intellectually deficient. To express them in rational form would not be difficult, but it would be wasteful of words. Nor is such paradox a merely wilful display of wit; it is an essential part of Emily's mode of expression. Her wit has been compared to the metaphysical style of Donne; it may also be compared with the gnomic style of Blake. It occurs in her letters and was, according to witnesses, a feature of her conversation. I doubt if she was ever merely clever, or riddled simply for effect. She riddled for truth which, as she said, "is such a rare thing. It is delightful to tell it." But it is sometimes embarrassing, especially amidst the minor dishonesties demanded by social convention. Emily's reply to Higginson at the end of their first interview, when he said he would come again "some time," punctured his little dishonesty without hurting him; perhaps at the time he did not even know what she meant: "say, in a long time; that will be nearer. Some time is no time."

Emily's arrival at the truth in this sibylline fashion is not so much irrational as super-rational. She was interested, not so much in a truth for its own sake—she was not a philosopher or a moralist—as in a direct vision of the truth. One might rationalize the vision or intuition after it had occurred, but that was not her business as a poet. In seeking to understand her poems, which are often highly cryptic, we require intuition rather than reason. In such a poem as *It dropped so low in my regard* Emily is indeed concerned with a moral observation, but she does not moralize.

> It dropped so low in my regard
> I heard it hit the ground
> And go to pieces on the stones
> At bottom of my mind;
>
> Yet blamed the fate that fractured less
> Than I reviled myself
> For entertaining plated wares
> Upon my silver shelf.

It is irrelevant to ask what "it" is. The point of the poem is not to rebuke the "it," whatever it is, for having appeared better than it was;

it is, rather, to make the moral observation that when we have over-estimated something, it is ourselves we blame for our initial lack of perception. An experience of self-reproach, such as this, had to be lived out, apprehended, and dismissed; it could not be dismissed until it had been given permanent embodiment in poetic form. Had Emily been primarily interested in moral observation, she would have written a prose treatise. But she was concerned with a different order of truth from the truth which is expressed in prose. If she was not a "professional poet," she had no other profession. The technique of writing poems, not as a rational art, but as significant "gesture" (to use Blackmur's word) was her constant preoccupation. On the technical side—in so far as she is allowed to have had any technique at all—she has been censured for three faults: bad grammar, bad rhymes, and irregular rhythms. The grammar of her letters is conventional enough, and it must be supposed that the "bad grammar" of the poems is deliberate, or at any rate justi-fied in her eyes by the demands of poetic form. It may be that she regarded formal grammatical consistency as of less importance than com-pression and economy of language. Her use of a sort of subjunctive mood has been frequently remarked on, and I think that it has to be explained on the ground that truth to her is often *provisional;* to one constitu-tionally timid, and scrupulously truthful, the subjunctive mood would come naturally. We may say that the use of the indicative implies con-fidence, the use of the subjunctive uncertainty.

> They say that time assuages.
> Time never did assuage.
> An actual suffering strengthens
> As sinews do, with age.
>
> Time is a test of trouble
> But not a remedy.
> If such it prove, it prove too
> There was no malady.

There is here a characteristic shift from the mood of confident asser-tion in the first stanza to that of uncertainty in the second; we may say, of course, that the second "prove" in the penultimate line is just careless. The American critic Yvor Winters[3] speaks of Emily's "habitual careless-

---

[3] *Maule's Curse*. New Directions, 1938. Like Blackmur Winters combines perfunctory praise ("She is one of the greatest lyric poets of all time") with a general attitude of severe disapproval. After quoting *I like to see it lap the miles* (No. 85), he says: "The poem is abominable; and the quality of silly playfulness which renders it abominable is diffused more or less perceptibly throughout most of her work . . ." I have given earlier my reasons for insisting that these weaker poems must be ignored—though I do not agree with what Winters says of *I like to see it lap the miles*.

ness." But since this sort of shift is so common, we should do well to consider whether it is not deliberate. Surely there may here be an elliptical suggestion of "will prove" or "may prove." The statement that the alleged healing power of time is an illusion is thus made less absolute. She is not committed to the judgement that a person who has been cured of a sorrow never really felt sorrow. Naturally the assertion would be stronger without the subjunctive, but it would be less honest. Emily wishes to explore moral truth, not to preach. There are also in plenty, especially during the period of Emily's greatest creative power, poems of confident assertion, strongly indicative in mood, like *Because I could not stop for death* (No. 103).

As for the irregularity of Emily's rhymes and rhythms, it is difficult to find any consistent explanation, or any principle in which they can be said to occur deliberately. Emily composed by instinct—which is not to say automatically. She used the basic rhythms of the hymns she had heard from childhood, adapting them to the need of the moment. Her instinct told her that mechanical regularity makes for monotony. Her rhythms, considered as personal variations on a rigid pattern, are to be justified, or found wanting, according to the shapes and sounds of particular poems. To my ear her rhythmic sense is seldom absolutely deficient, often inspired. There is more variety than the formal appearance of the poems would suggest, and a study of the rhythmic variations in any half-dozen of her best poems would reveal considerable subtlety.

Attempts have been made to show that her use of assonance instead of full rhyme is always deliberate artistry. It would be truer to say that, on the whole though not invariably, full rhyme accompanies her moods of confidence, and assonance her moods of uncertainty. But the exceptions are significant. All we can say is that she felt no particular compulsion to find exact rhymes, and that probably assonance also helped her to get away from the mechanical jingle of hymn-forms.

Some may be satisfied to condemn what they call her "carelessness," or to say that she had no technique, or to regard her stylistic irregularities as a proof of eccentricity or amateurishness. I prefer to say that there are many possible causes for poetic failure, and that technical inadequacy is not the most important. A feeble poem is not redeemed by exact rhymes, correct grammar and rhythmical regularity. Not all the technical elegance of, say, Austin Dobson's *vers de société* can bring it to life: on the contrary, the craftsmanship only serves to emphasise the essential emptiness. Emily was concerned with the realization of a vision or a truth in language—the right word took priority over technical conformity. When she was wholly inspired, technique, as it were, rose to the occasion; when she was not, technique failed as well as language. Emily had no excess of technical ease with which to disguise a central failure of inspiration. It would be idle to deny that there are technical blemishes which Emily herself, had she had the benefit of sound advice and the desire to perfect her poems for public inspection, would have wished to correct. But we must take her poems for what they are: if any are good, they are technically good. There is no such thing as a good poem which is technically bad. We have to do with a poet of almost total originality, and it is very rarely that originality and formal perfection go together. There is about all original poets—Skelton, Donne, Blake, Hardy, Hopkins—a certain home-made roughness of form which, according to temperament, some will regard as a blessing, and some as a blemish. Ben Jonson regarded Donne's metrical irregularity as a blemish, and on the whole posterity has disagreed with Jonson.

It is when we come to look at Emily's ideas, and the language in which she expresses them, that we are most struck by her originality and her audacity. To read, for instance *A bird came down the walk* (No. 52) is to feel that we have never seen a bird before—or rather, that we have never noticed the birds we constantly see.

> He glanced with rapid eyes
> That hurried all around;
> They looked like frightened beads, I thought.

Here, the faithful realization of the state of perpetual insecurity in which a bird lives owes everything to a primitive act of self-identification with the bird. It is as if Emily's own timidity were dissolved in the bird's. It is subjectivity carried to the point of self-annihilation. We are reminded of Keats' sparrow picking about among the gravel. I cannot follow a critic who calls Emily sophisticated. She had, at such moments as these, a purely primitive vision; there is nothing of the *faux naïf* in her descriptive writing.

There is in this poem a certain cool brilliance, a certain hard objectivity of outward appearance which is often revealed when the poet is in fact most engaged. She lived her poems, and never simply thought them; they were paid for in sensibility or in suffering or in ecstasy. She had many costly failures, but no cheap successes. In *The last night that she lived* (No. 140) it is evident that the poet is acutely involved, and for that reason she is careful to overstate nothing: the poem begins almost casually. In comparison with most conventional elegies its tone is off-hand. Then, with the utmost economy of language, the changing emotions of the watchers are described as the moment of death approaches. When the moment comes, the watchers are temporarily ignored: four lines are given to the supreme instant—

> She mentioned, and forgot;
> Then lightly as a reed
> Bent to the water, struggled scarce,
> Consented, and was dead.

The simile in the second and third lines is chosen with a skill or insight which cannot be analysed—we recall that to Emily water was usually a symbol of eternity. Then in the final stanza the unspoken feelings of the onlookers are again expressed. I doubt if a deathbed has ever been more indelibly realized in words. Emily's own phrase "a nearness to tremendousness" comes to mind; always when she is nearest to tremendousness she speaks most quietly. At the deathbed the feeling of awe is uppermost: the sense of loss will come later, but for the present all purely human feeling is numbed. One has to go back to *The Lyke-Wake Dirge* to find anything so deliberately impressive in its holding back of the forces of dissolution and annihilation. After reading such a poem as this, one does not speak of technique.

When she appears most cool, most off-hand, most nearly approaching flippancy, we should be especially on our guard against missing her profoundest significances. It is difficult to say exactly what experience is recorded in the extraordinary and tantalizing poem *I started early, took my dog* (No. 76). It is evident that here the sea represents some overwhelming force, of great destructive power—death possibly, or love, or perhaps both. To ships on the sea the poet appears to be a mouse—symbol of timidity. What begins in a playful vein concludes as a pursuit to the death. It is only when she reaches the solid familiarity of home, the reassurance of the town she knows so well, that the pursuit ends.

Such a poem as this holds a kind of compulsion not to be explained by anything we can be sure it means. Far more comprehensible, but no less mysterious, is *Because I could not stop for death* (No. 103). This is one of the best of those poems in which Emily triumphs over death by accepting it, calmly, civilly, as befits a gentlewoman receiving the attentions of a gentleman. It is an essay in death-in-life. Only by civilizing death and by familiarizing herself with it can it be brought within the scheme of what is tolerable and credible. The tone is tenderly ironic, the atmosphere tinged with sorrow for life and concern for the smallness of the human soul that must face inexorable death, solitary except for its immortality. The poem is simple, almost commonplace, yet the mystery that pervades it is inexhaustible. There is, within this mystery, a sense of reconciliation. To find anything like it we have to go to Prospero's closing speeches in *The Tempest*.

In order to apprehend, if not to understand, the sources of Emily Dickinson's mystery, we have to consider her language. It would be a long and rewarding study to examine Emily's use of words in constructing the world in which she lived out her poems. There is no room here for such a study, but the following passage from Allen Tate's essay would form a valuable starting-point.

The two elements of her style, considered as a point of view, are immortality, or the idea of permanence, and the physical process of death or decay. Her diction has two corresponding features: words of Latin or Greek origin and, sharply opposed to these, the concrete Saxon element. It is this verbal conflict that gives to her verse its high tension; it is not a device deliberately seized upon, but a feeling for language that senses out the two fundamental components of English and their metaphysical relation: the Latin for ideas and the Saxon for perceptions—the peculiar virtue of English as a poetic language.

This applies to all poets writing in English who have a true insight into the nature of their medium. Yet not all poets, endowed as they were with this uniquely poetic medium, have recognized its peculiar quality. Shakespeare undoubtedly did:

> If thou didst ever hold me in thy heart,
> Absent thee from felicity awhile,
> And in this harsh world draw thy breath in pain,
> To tell my story.

The dignity of abstract ideas is here combined and contrasted with the pathos of simple human suffering to achieve that balance of intellect and senses which is fundamental to the apprehension of life in poetic terms. It is in lines like these that we find, if anywhere, the *meaning* of life. Possibly Emily learned the secret from Shakespeare, whom she read constantly. At all events this Shakespearean accent, the balance between the abstract quality of Romance words and the concrete actuality of the Saxon, is never far from her poetry at its finest.

"Sumptuous Destitution"

by Richard Wilbur

At some point Emily Dickinson sent her whole Calvinist vocabulary into exile, telling it not to come back until it would subserve her own sense of things.

Of course, that is not a true story, but it is a way of saying what I find most remarkable in Emily Dickinson. She inherited a great and overbearing vocabulary which, had she used it submissively, would have forced her to express an established theology and psychology. But she would not let that vocabulary write her poems for her. There lies the real difference between a poet like Emily Dickinson and a fine versifier like Isaac Watts. To be sure, Emily Dickinson also wrote in the metres of hymnody, and paraphrased the Bible, and made her poems turn on great words like Immortality and Salvation and Election. But in her poems those great words are not merely being themselves; they have been adopted, for expressive purposes; they have been taken personally, and therefore redefined.

The poems of Emily Dickinson are a continual appeal to experience, motivated by an arrogant passion for the truth. "Truth is so rare a thing," she once said, "it is delightful to tell it." And, sending some poems to Colonel Higginson, she wrote, "Excuse them, if they are untrue." And again, to the same correspondent, she observed, "Candor is the only wile" —meaning that the writer's bag of tricks need contain one trick only, the trick of being honest. That her taste for truth involved a regard for objective fact need not be argued: we have her poem on the snake, and that on the hummingbird, and they are small masterpieces of exact description. She liked accuracy; she liked solid and homely detail; and even in her most exalted poems we are surprised and reassured by buckets, shawls, or buzzing flies.

But her chief truthfulness lay in her insistence on discovering the facts of her inner experience. She was a Linnaeus to the phenomena of her own consciousness, describing and distinguishing the states and motions

"Sumptuous Destitution" by Richard Wilbur. From *Emily Dickinson: Three Views* (Amherst: Amherst College Press, 1960) by Richard Wilbur, Louise Bogan, and Archibald MacLeish. Copyright © 1960 by the Amherst College Press. Reprinted by permission of the author and Amherst College Press.

of her soul. The results of this "psychic reconnaissance," as Professor
Whicher called it, were several. For one thing, it made her articulate
about inward matters which poetry had never so sharply defined; specifically, it made her capable of writing two such lines as these:

> A perfect, paralyzing bliss
> Contented as despair.

We often assent to the shock of a paradox before we understand it, but
those lines are so just and so concentrated as to explode their meaning
instantly in the mind. They did not come so easily, I think, to Emily
Dickinson. Unless I guess wrongly as to chronology, such lines were the
fruit of long poetic research; the poet had worked toward them through
much study of the way certain emotions can usurp consciousness entirely,
annulling our sense of past and future, cancelling near and far, con-
verting all time and space to a joyous or grievous here and now. It is in
their ways of annihilating time and space that bliss and despair are comparable.

Which leads me to a second consequence of Emily Dickinson's self-
analysis. It is one thing to assert as pious doctrine that the soul has power,
with God's grace, to master circumstance. It is another thing to find out
personally, as Emily Dickinson did in writing her psychological poems,
that the aspect of the world is in no way constant, that the power of
external things depends on our state of mind, that the soul selects its own
society and may, if granted strength to do so, select a superior order and
scope of consciousness which will render it finally invulnerable. She
learned these things by witnessing her own courageous spirit.

Another result of Emily Dickinson's introspection was that she discovered some grounds, in the nature of her soul and its affections, for a
personal conception of such ideas as Heaven and Immortality, and so
managed a precarious convergence between her inner experience and her
religious inheritance. What I want to attempt now is a rough sketch of
the imaginative logic by which she did this. I had better say before I
start that I shall often seem demonstrably wrong, because Emily Dickinson, like many poets, was consistent in her concerns but inconsistent in
her attitudes. The following, therefore, is merely an opinion as to her
main drift.

Emily Dickinson never lets us forget for very long that in some respects
life gave her short measure; and indeed it is possible to see the greater
part of her poetry as an effort to cope with her sense of privation. I think
that for her there were three major privations: she was deprived of an
orthodox and steady religious faith; she was deprived of love; she was
deprived of literary recognition.

At the age of 17, after a series of revival meetings at Mount Holyoke

Seminary, Emily Dickinson found that she must refuse to become a professing Christian. To some modern minds this may seem to have been a sensible and necessary step; and surely it was a step toward becoming such a poet as she became. But for her, no pleasure in her own integrity could then eradicate the feeling that she had betrayed a deficiency, a want of grace. In her letters to Abiah Root she tells of the enhancing effect of conversion on her fellow-students, and says of herself in a famous passage:

> *I* am one of the lingering bad ones, and so do I slink away, and pause and ponder, and ponder and pause, and do work without knowing why, not surely, for this brief world, and more sure it is not for heaven, and I ask what this message *means* that they ask for so very eagerly: *you* know of this depth and fulness, will you try to tell me about it?

There is humor in that, and stubbornness, and a bit of characteristic lurking pride: but there is also an anguished sense of having separated herself, through some dry incapacity, from spiritual community, from purpose, and from magnitude of life. As a child of evangelical Amherst, she inevitably thought of purposive, heroic life as requiring a vigorous faith. Out of such a thought she later wrote:

> The abdication of Belief
> Makes the Behavior small—
> Better an ignis fatuus
> Than no illume at all—(1551)

That hers *was* a species of religious personality goes without saying; but by her refusal of such ideas as original sin, redemption, hell, and election, she made it impossible for herself—as Professor Whicher observed—"to share the religious life of her generation." She became an unsteady congregation of one.

Her second privation, the privation of love, is one with which her poems and her biographies have made us exceedingly familiar, though some biographical facts remain conjectural. She had the good fortune, at least once, to bestow her heart on another; but she seems to have found her life, in great part, a history of loneliness, separation, and bereavement.

As for literary fame, some will deny that Emily Dickinson ever greatly desired it, and certainly there is evidence, mostly from her latter years, to support such a view. She *did* write that "Publication is the auction/Of the mind of man." And she *did* say to Helen Hunt Jackson, "How can you print a piece of your soul?" But earlier, in 1861, she had frankly expressed to Sue Dickinson the hope that "sometime" she might make her kinfolk proud of her. The truth is, I think, that Emily Dickinson knew she was good, and began her career with a normal appetite for recognition. I think that she later came, with some reason, to despair of being understood or properly valued, and so directed against her hopes of fame what was by then a well-developed disposition to renounce. That she wrote a good number of poems about fame supports my view: the subjects to which a poet returns are those which vex him.

What did Emily Dickinson do, as a poet, with her sense of privation? One thing she quite often did was to pose as the laureate and attorney of the empty-handed, and question God about the economy of His creation. Why, she asked, is a fatherly God so sparing of His presence? Why is there never a sign that prayers are heard? Why does Nature tell us no comforting news of its Maker? Why do some receive a whole loaf, while others must starve on a crumb? Where is the benevolence in shipwreck and earthquake? By asking such questions as these, she turned complaint into critique, and used her own sufferings as experiential evidence about the nature of the deity. The God who emerges from these poems is a God who does not answer, an unrevealed God whom one cannot confidently approach through Nature or through doctrine.

But there was another way in which Emily Dickinson dealt with her sentiment of lack—another emotional strategy which was both more frequent and more fruitful. I refer to her repeated assertion of the paradox that privation is more plentiful than plenty; that to renounce is to possess the more; that "The Banquet of abstemiousness/Defaces that of wine." We all know how the poet illustrated this ascetic paradox in her behavior —how in her latter years she chose to live in relative retirement, keeping the world, even in its dearest aspects, at a physical remove. She would write her friends, telling them how she missed them, then flee upstairs when they came to see her; afterward, she might send a note of apology, offering the odd explanation that "We shun because we prize." Any reader of Dickinson biographies can furnish other examples, dramatic or homely, of this prizing and shunning, this yearning and renouncing: in my own mind's eye is a picture of Emily Dickinson watching a gay circus caravan from the distance of her chamber window.

In her inner life, as well, she came to keep the world's images, even the images of things passionately desired, at the remove which renunciation makes; and her poetry at its most mature continually proclaims that to lose or forego what we desire is somehow to gain. We may say, if we like, with some of the poet's commentators, that this central paradox of her thought is a rationalization of her neurotic plight; but we had better add that it is also a discovery of something about the soul. Let me read you a little poem of psychological observation which, whatever its date of composition, may logically be considered as an approach to that discovery.

> Undue Significance a starving man attaches
> To Food—
> Far off—He sighs—and therefore—Hopeless—
> And therefore—Good—

Partaken—it relieves—indeed—
But proves us
That Spices fly
In the Receipt—It was the Distance—
Was Savory—(439)

This poem describes an educational experience, in which a starving man is brought to distinguish between appetite and desire. So long as he despairs of sustenance, the man conceives it with the eye of desire as infinitely delicious. But when, after all, he secures it and appeases his hunger, he finds that its imagined spices have flown. The moral is plain: once an object has been magnified by desire, it cannot be wholly possessed by appetite.

The poet is not concerned, in this poem, with passing any judgment. She is simply describing the way things go in the human soul, telling us that the frustration of appetite awakens or abets desire, and that the effect of intense desiring is to render any finite satisfaction disappointing. Now I want to read you another well-known poem, in which Emily Dickinson was again considering privation and possession, and the modes of enjoyment possible to each. In this case, I think, a judgment is strongly implied.

Success is counted sweetest
By those who ne'er succeed.
To comprehend a nectar
Requires sorest need.

Not one of all the purple Host
Who took the Flag today
Can tell the definition
So clear of Victory

As he defeated—dying—
On whose forbidden ear
The distant strains of triumph
Burst agonized and clear! (67)

Certainly Emily Dickinson's critics are right in calling this poem an expression of the idea of compensation—of the idea that every evil confers some balancing good, that through bitterness we learn to appreciate the sweet, that "Water is taught by thirst." The defeated and dying soldier of this poem is compensated by a greater awareness of the meaning of victory than the victors themselves can have: he can comprehend the joy of success through its polar contrast to his own despair.

The poem surely does say that; yet it seems to me that there is something further implied. On a first reading, we are much impressed with the wretchedness of the dying soldier's lot, and an improved understanding of the nature of victory may seem small compensation for defeat and death; but the more one ponders this poem the likelier it grows that Emily Dickinson is arguing the *superiority* of defeat to victory, of frustration to satisfaction, and of anguished comprehension to mere possession. What do the victors have but victory, a victory which they cannot fully savor or clearly define? They have paid for their triumph by a sacrifice of awareness; a material gain has cost them a spiritual loss. For the dying soldier, the case is reversed: defeat and death are attended by an increase of awareness, and material loss has led to spiritual gain. Emily Dickinson would think that the better bargain.

In the first of these two poems I have read, it was possible to imagine the poet as saying that a starving man's visions of food are but wish fulfillments, and hence illusory; but the second poem assures us of the contrary —assures us that food, or victory, or any other good thing is best comprehended by the eye of desire from the vantage of privation. We must now ask in what way desire can define things, what comprehension of nectars it can have beyond a sense of inaccessible sweetness.

Since Emily Dickinson was not a philosopher, and never set forth her thought in any orderly way, I shall answer that question by a quotation from the seventeenth-century divine Thomas Traherne. Conveniently for us, Traherne is thinking, in this brief meditation, about food—specifically, about acorns—as perceived by appetite and by desire.

> The services of things and their excellencies are spiritual: being objects not of the eye, but of the mind: and you more spiritual by how much more you esteem them. Pigs eat acorns, but neither consider the sun that gave them life, nor the influences of the heavens by which they were nourished, nor the very root of the tree from whence they came. This being the work of Angels, who in a wide and clear light see even the sea that gave them moisture: And feed upon that acorn spiritually while they know the ends for which it was created, and feast upon all these as upon a World of Joys within it: while to ignorant swine that eat the shell, it is an empty husk of no taste nor delightful savor.

Emily Dickinson could not have written that, for various reasons, a major reason being that she could not see in Nature any revelations of divine purpose. But like Traherne she discovered that the soul has an infinite hunger, a hunger to possess all things. (That discovery, I suspect, was the major fruit of her introspection.) And like Traherne she distinguished two ways of possessing things, the way of appetite and the way of desire. What Traherne said of the pig she said of her favorite insect:

> Auto da Fe and Judgment—
> Are nothing to the Bee—
> His separation from His Rose—
> To Him—sums Misery—(620)

The creature of appetite (whether insect or human) pursues satisfaction, and strives to possess the object in itself; it cannot imagine the vaster economy of desire, in which the pain of abstinence is justified by moments of infinite joy, and the object is spiritually possessed, not merely for itself, but more truly as an index of the All. That is how one comprehends a nectar. Miss Dickinson's bee does not comprehend the rose which it plunders, because the truer sweetness of the rose lies beyond the rose, in its relationship to the whole of being; but she would say that Gerard Manley Hopkins comprehends a bluebell when, having noticed its intrinsic beauties, he adds, "I know the beauty of Our Lord by it." And here is an eight-line poem of her own, in which she comprehends the full sweetness of water.

> We thirst at first—'tis Nature's Act—
> And later—when we die—
> A little Water supplicate—
> Of fingers going by—
>
> It intimates the finer want—
> Whose adequate supply
> Is that Great Water in the West—
> Termed Immortality— (726)

Emily Dickinson elected the economy of desire, and called her privation good, rendering it positive by renunciation. And so she came to live in a huge world of delectable distances. Far-off words like "Brazil" or "Circassian" appear continually in her poems as symbols of things distanced by loss or renunciation, yet infinitely prized and yearned-for. So identified in her mind are distance and delight that, when ravished by the sight of a hummingbird in her garden, she calls it "the mail from Tunis." And not only are the objects of her desire distant; they are also very often moving away, their sweetness increasing in proportion to their remoteness. "To disappear enhances," one of the poems begins, and another closes with these lines:

> The Mountain—at a given distance—
> In Amber—lies—
> Approached—the Amber flits—a little—
> And That's—the Skies— (572)

To the eye of desire, all things are seen in a profound perspective, either moving or gesturing toward the vanishing-point. Or to use a figure which may be closer to Miss Dickinson's thought, to the eye of desire the world is a centrifuge, in which all things are straining or flying toward the occult circumference. In some such way, Emily Dickinson conceived her world, and it was in a spatial metaphor that she gave her personal definition of Heaven. "Heaven," she said, "is what I cannot reach."

At times it seems that there is nothing in her world but her own soul, with its attendant abstractions, and, at a vast remove, the inscrutable Heaven. On most of what might intervene she has closed the valves of her attention, and what mortal objects she does acknowledge are riddled by desire to the point of transparency. Here is a sentence from her correspondence: "Enough is of so vast a sweetness, I suppose it never occurs, only pathetic counterfeits." The writer of that sentence could not invest her longings in any finite object. Again she wrote, "Emblem is immeasurable—that is why it is better than fulfilment, which can be drained." For such a sensibility, it was natural and necessary that things be touched with infinity. Therefore her nature poetry, when most serious, does not play descriptively with birds or flowers but presents us repeatedly with dawn, noon, and sunset, those grand ceremonial moments of the day which argue the splendor of Paradise. Or it shows us the ordinary landscape transformed by the electric brilliance of a storm; or it shows us the fields succumbing to the annual mystery of death. In her love-poems, Emily Dickinson was at first covetous of the beloved himself; indeed, she could be idolatrous, going so far as to say that his face, should she see it again in Heaven, would eclipse the face of Jesus. But in what I take to be her later work the beloved's lineaments, which were never very distinct, vanish entirely; he becomes pure emblem, a symbol of remote spiritual joy, and so is all but absorbed into the idea of Heaven. The lost beloved is, as one poem declares, "infinite when gone," and in such lines as the following we are aware of him mainly as an instrument in the poet's commerce with the beyond.

> Of all the Souls that stand create—
> I have elected—One—
> When Sense from Spirit—files away—
> And Subterfuge—is done—
> When that which is—and that which was—
> Apart—intrinsic—stand—
> And this brief Tragedy of Flesh—
> Is shifted—like a Sand—
> When Figures show their royal Front—
> And Mists—are carved away,
> Behold the Atom—I preferred—
> To all the lists of Clay! (664)

In this extraordinary poem, the corporeal beloved is seen as if from another and immaterial existence, and in such perspective his earthly person is but an atom of clay. His risen spirit, we presume, is more imposing, but it is certainly not in focus. What the rapt and thudding lines

of this poem portray is the poet's own magnificence of soul—her fidelity
to desire, her confidence of Heaven, her contempt of the world. Like
Cleopatra's final speeches, this poem is an irresistible demonstration of
spiritual status, in which the supernatural is so royally demanded that
skepticism is disarmed. A part of its effect derives, by the way, from the
fact that the life to come is described in an ambiguous present tense, so
that we half-suppose the speaker to be already in Heaven.

There were times when Emily Dickinson supposed this of herself, and
I want to close by making a partial guess at the logic of her claims to
beatitude. It seems to me that she generally saw Heaven as a kind of
infinitely remote bank, in which, she hoped, her untouched felicities were
drawing interest. Parting, she said, was all she knew of it. Hence it is
surprising to find her saying, in some poems, that Heaven has drawn near
to her, and that in her soul's "superior instants" Eternity has disclosed to
her "the colossal substance/Of immortality." Yet the contradiction can
be understood, if we recall what sort of evidence was persuasive to Emily
Dickinson.

"Too much of proof," she wrote, "affronts belief"; and she was little
convinced either by doctrine or by theological reasoning. Her residual
Calvinism was criticized and fortified by her study of her own soul in
action, and from the phenomena of her soul she was capable of making
the boldest inferences. That the sense of time is subject to the moods of
the soul seemed to her a proof of the soul's eternity. Her intensity of grief
for the dead, and her feeling of their continued presence, seemed to her
arguments for the reunion of souls in Heaven. And when she found in
herself infinite desires, "immortal longings," it seemed to her possible that
such desires might somewhere be infinitely answered.

One psychic experience which she interpreted as beatitude was "glee,"
or as some would call it, euphoria. Now, a notable thing about glee or
euphoria is its gratuitousness. It seems to come from nowhere, and it was
this apparent sourcelessness of the emotion from which Emily Dickinson
made her inference. "The 'happiness' without a cause," she said, "is the
best happiness, for glee intuitive and lasting is the gift of God." Having
foregone all earthly causes of happiness, she could only explain her glee,
when it came, as a divine gift—a compensation in joy for what she had
renounced in satisfaction, and a foretaste of the mood of Heaven. The
experience of glee, as she records it, is boundless: all distances collapse,
and the soul expands to the very circumference of things. Here is how she
put it in one of her letters: "Abroad is close tonight and I have but to
lift my hands to touch the 'Hights of Abraham.'" And one of her gleeful
poems begins,

> 'Tis little—I could care for Pearls—
> Who own the ample sea—

How often she felt that way we cannot know, and it hardly matters. As Robert Frost has pointed out, happiness can make up in height for what it lacks in length; and the important thing for us, as for her, is that she construed the experience as a divine gift. So also she thought of the power to write poetry, a power which, as we know, came to her often; and poetry must have been the chief source of her sense of blessedness. The poetic impulses which visited her seemed "bulletins from Immortality," and by their means she converted all her losses into gains, and all the pains of her life to that clarity and repose which were to her the qualities of Heaven. So superior did she feel, as a poet, to earthly circumstance, and so strong was her faith in words, that she more than once presumed to view this life from the vantage of the grave.

In a manner of speaking, she *was* dead. And yet her poetry, with its articulate faithfulness to inner and outer truth, its insistence on maximum consciousness, is not an avoidance of life but an eccentric mastery of it. Let me close by reading you a last poem, in which she conveys both the extent of her repudiation and the extent of her happiness.

> The Missing All, prevented Me
> From missing minor Things.
> If nothing larger than a World's
> Departure from a Hinge
> Or Sun's extinction, be observed
> 'Twas not so large that I
> Could lift my Forehead from my work
> For Curiosity. (985)

A Mystical Poet

by Louise Bogan

It has been suggested that I develop, on this occasion, a statement I made in 1945, in an article published in that year—that the time had come "to assess Emily Dickinson's powers on the highest level of mystical poetry, where they should be assessed." Since then, the appearance of the *Collected Poems* and of the *Collected Letters*, superbly edited by Thomas H. Johnson, has made such an assessment less difficult than it formerly had to be. For now, with the existence of these definitive works, the stages of the poet's development are connected and clarified. We are now faced, as we should be, with the career of a writer who—we now realize—throughout her life made the most difficult kind of choices, many directed toward the protection of her sensitive nature and of her remarkable poetic gift. It is the poet Dickinson who has advanced into the full light of literary history and now belongs not only to Amherst, not only to America, but to the world that reads her either in English or in translation.

Now, the term "mystical poetry" is a difficult one to deal with. The words "mystic" and "mysticism" have become rather suspect in modern, materialist society. So it is important to define and place this term, at the outset. Mystics have appeared, it would seem, with fair frequency at many periods, in many cultures; but there is no doubt that when, in the West, we speak of true mysticism, we have in mind the example of the Christian saints. "In Christianity," says Evelyn Underhill, "the 'natural mysticism' . . . which is latent in humanity and at a certain point of development breaks out in every race, came to itself; and attributed for the first time true and distinct personality to its Object"—namely, God. True mystics do not indulge in diffuse pantheism or hold to the aim of "the occult," which wishes to wrench supernal power to human uses. In the words of another commentator: "The aim and content of Christian mysticism is not self or nature, but God."

We can see at once that there is a difference between the character, as well as the aims, of true mystics and of poets; and we know that to come upon the two gifts in one person is extremely rare. But close points of resemblance do exist between the mystic experience, at its purest and best, and the experience of poetic—or indeed, any creative—expression. Poets down the centuries, visited by that power which the ancients call *the Muse,* have described their experience in much the same way as the mystic describes his ecstatic union with Divine Truth. This experience has been rendered at length, and dramatically, by Dante, as well as by St. John of the Cross; and certain poems in the literature of every language attest to moments when, for the poet, "the deep and primal life which he shares with all creation has been roused from its sleep." And both poets and mystics have described with great poignance that sense of deprivation and that shutting away from grace which follows the loss of the vision (or of the inspiring breath), which is called, in the language of mysticism, "the dark night of the soul."

Certainly one of the triumphs brought about by the emergence of the Romantic spirit, in English poetry, at the end of the eighteenth century, was a freeing and an enlargement of poetic vision, and in the nineteenth century we come upon a multiplication of poets whose spiritual perceptions were acute. Beyond Vaughan and Herbert (who, in the seventeenth century, worked from a religious base) we think of Blake, of the young Wordsworth; of Keats and Shelley; of Emily Brontë; of Gerard Manley Hopkins; and we can extend the list into our own day with the names of Yeats and T. S. Eliot. By examining the work of these poets—to whom the imagination, the creative spirit of man, was of utmost importance—we find that the progress of the mystic toward illumination, and of the poet toward the full depth and richness of his insight—are much alike. Both work from the world of reality, toward the realm of Essence; from the microcosm to the macrocosm. Both have an intense and accurate sense of their surroundings; there is nothing vague or floating in their perception of reality; it is indeed as though they saw "through, not with, the eye." And they are filled with love for the beauty they perceive in the world of time—"this remarkable world" as Emily Dickinson called it; and concerning death they are neither fearful nor morbid—how could they be, since they feel immortality behind it? They document life's fearful limitations from which they suffer, but they do not mix self-pity with the account of their suffering (which they describe, like their joy, in close detail). They see the world in a grain of sand and Heaven in a wild flower; and now and again they bring eternity into focus, as it were, in a phrase of the utmost clarity. In the work of Emily Dickinson such moments of still and halted perception are many. The slant of light on a winter day, the still brilliance of a summer noon, the sound of the wind before the rain—she speaks of these, and we share the shock of insight, the slight dislocation of serial events, the sudden shift from the Manifold into the One.

One of the dominant facts concerning Emily Dickinson is her spirit of

religious unorthodoxy. Her deeply religious feeling ran outside the
bounds of dogma; this individualism was, in fact, an inheritance from her
Calvinist forbears, but it was out of place when contrasted to the Evan-
gelicanism to which, in her time, so many Protestants had succumbed.
She early set herself against the guilt and gloom inherent in this reviv-
alism. She avoided the constrictions which a narrow insistence on religious
rule and law would put upon her. She had read Emerson with delight,
but, as Yvor Winters has remarked, it is a mistake to think of her as a
Transcendentalist in dimity. Here again she worked through to a standpoint and an interpretation of her own; her attitude toward pain and
suffering, toward the shocking facts of existence, was far more realistic
than Emerson's. As we examine her chief spiritual preoccupations, we
see how closely she relates to the English Romantic poets who, a generation or so before her, fought a difficult and unpopular battle against the
eighteenth century's cold logic and mechanical point of view. The names
of Blake and Coleridge come to mind; we know that to both these poets
the cold theory of Locke represented "a deadly heresy on the nature of
existence." It is difficult to look back to this period of early Romantic
breakthrough, since so much of that early boldness and originality was
later dissipated in excesses of various kinds. But it is important to remember that Blake attached the greatest importance to the human imagination as an aspect of some mystery beyond the human, and to listen
to his ringing words: "The world of Imagination is the world of Eternity.
. . . The world of Imagination is Infinite and Eternal, whereas the world
of generation is Finite and Temporal . . ."—and to remember, as well,
that "Blake, Wordsworth, Coleridge, Shelley and Keats shared the belief
that the imagination was nothing less than God as he operates in the
human soul." C. M. Bowra, writing of the Romantic ethos in general,
brings out a fact which has been generally overlooked: that, although
Romantic poetry became a European phenomenon, English Romantic
poetry "almost alone . . . connected visionary insight with a superior
order of being." "There is hardly a trace of this [insight]," Bowra goes on
to say, "in Hugo, or Heine or Lermontov. They have their full share of
longing, but almost nothing of Romantic vision. . . ." Hölderlin, in
Germany tried to share a lost vision of Greece, but on the whole it was
the English who accomplished a transformation in thought and emotion
"for which there is no parallel in their age." It is surely in the company
of these English poets that Emily Dickinson belongs. At its most intense,
her vision not only matched, but transcended theirs; she crossed the same
boundaries with a like intransigence; and the same vigorous flowers sprang
from different seeds, in the spirit of a woman born in 1830, in New England, in America.

The drawing of close parallels between the life and circumstances of
poets is often an unrewarding task. But in the case of Emily Dickinson
because hers was for so long considered a particularly isolated career, it

is interesting to make certain comparisons. It has been pointed out that
there is a close resemblance between the lives, temperament and works of
Emily Brontë and Emily Dickinson. And one or two resemblances between Emily Dickinson and Blake (Blake taken as a lyric poet rather than
as a prophet) can be traced (quite apart from the fairly unimportant fact
that Miss Dickinson, in her apprenticeship, closely imitated Blake's form
in at least two poems). Both took over the simplest forms of the song and
the hymn and turned this simplicity to their own uses. Both seemed to
work straight from almost dictated inspiration (Blake, indeed, claimed
that his poems were dictated to him intact and entire) but we now know,
from an examination of their manuscripts, that both worked over their
original drafts with meticulous care. Both had to struggle against hamper-
ing circumstances: Blake against poverty and misunderstanding, and
Dickinson against a lack of true response in the traditionally stiffened
society in which she found herself. To both poets, limitation and boundary finally yielded originality and power; they were sufficiently outside
the spirit of their times so that they were comparatively untouched by
the vagaries of fashion; they both were able to wring from solitary contemplation sound working principles and just form. T. S. Eliot, in his
essay on Blake, speaks of Blake's peculiarity "which can be seen to be the
peculiarity of all great poetry. . . . It is merely a peculiar honesty, which,
in a world frightened to be honest, is particularly terrifying. It is an
honesty against which the whole world conspires, because it is unpleasant.
Blake's poetry has the unpleasantness of great poetry. Nothing that can
be called abnormal or perverse, none of the things which exemplify the
sickness of an epoch or a fashion, have this quality; only those things
which, by some extraordinary labor of simplification, exhibit the essential
sickness or strength of the human soul." Eliot then remarks that the question about Blake the man "is a question of the circumstances that concurred to permit this honesty in his work. . . . The favoring conditions
probably include these two: that, early apprenticed to a manual occupa-
tion, he was not compelled to acquire any other education in literature
than he wanted, or to acquire it for any other reason than he wanted it; and
that, being a humble engraver, he had no journalistic-social career open
to him. There was, that is to say, nothing to distract him from his interests
or to corrupt these interests—neither . . . the standards of society, nor
the temptation of success; nor was he exposed to imitation of himself or
anyone else. . . . These circumstances are what make him innocent."

The circumstances which led to Emily Dickinson's very nearly complete
seclusion are, of course, different from those which Eliot mentions as
applying to Blake. It was physical frailty which put an end to her formal
education. But later, as we read the record of her withdrawal, as this
record appears in the *Letters* (and, of course, the full reasons are not
given) we can detect the element of choice working. By the time she
wrote to Higginson in 1862 she had made that choice, and only wanted

to have it confirmed. She wished to know whether or not her poems were "alive"—if they "breathed." She received a certain confirmation that they were and did; and she kept to her solitude. This solitude was not harsh. Her love for her friends never diminished, nor her delight in their occasional presence; her family ties were strong; her daily round sustained her; and the joy she felt in the natural world—particularly in flowers and in children—continued. Until a series of tragedies (beginning with the death of her father) began to break down her spiritual balance, she held to that balance over a long period of years. Balance, delicacy and force—fed by her exquisite senses and her infinitely lively and inquisitive mind—these are the qualities which reinforce her vision into the heart and spirit of nature, and into her own heart.

An added pleasure is given us, as we read Emily Dickinson's poetry from beginning to end, by the openness and inclusiveness of the work. Every sort of poem has been preserved; no strict process of self-editing has taken place, and we are not faced with periods in which much has been suppressed. The failures and the successes stand side by side; the poems expressing the poet's more childish and undeveloped characteristics and the poems upon which the sentimentality of her time left its mark, are often followed or preceded by poems which define and express the very nearly indefinable and inexpressible. There is no professionalism, in the worst sense, here; and it is interesting to note that, although she sought out Higginson's advice and named herself his "scholar," she never altered a poem of hers according to any suggestion of his. She had, at one time, perhaps been willing to be published, but, later, she could do without print.

We have, then, in Johnson's edition of the poems published in 1955, as complete a record of the development of a lyric talent as exists in literature. Scholars have busied themselves with the record; we know what color she names most frequently (purple) and what books she read (Shakespeare and the Bible well in the lead). We ourselves can discover, in the index to the three volumes, that her favorite subject was not death, as was long supposed; for life, love, and the soul are also recurring subjects. But the greatest interest lies in her progress as a writer, and as a person. We see the young poet moving away, by gradual degrees, from her early slight addiction to graveyardism, to an Emersonian belief in the largeness and harmony of nature. Step by step, she advances into the terror and anguish of her destiny; she is frightened, but she holds fast and describes her fright. She is driven to the verge of sanity, but manages to remain, in some fashion, the observer and recorder of her extremity. Nature is no longer a friend, but often an inimical presence. Nature is a haunted house. And—a truth even more terrible—the inmost self can be haunted.

At the highest summit of her art, she resembles no one. She begins to cast forward toward the future: to produce poems in which we recognize, as one French critic has said, both the *voyant* faculty of Rimbaud and

Mallarmé's feeling for the mystery and sacredness of the word. This high period begins in the early 1860s, and is not entirely consistent; the power seems to come and go, but it is indubitably there. And when it is present, she can describe with clinical precision the actual emotional event, the supreme moment of anguish, and even her own death itself. And she finds symbols which fit the event—terrible symbols. The experience of suffering is like dying of the cold; or it resembles the approach of a maelstrom, which finally engulfs the victim; one escapes from suffering as from the paws of a fiend, from whose grasp one emerges more dead than alive. One poem, written about 1863, defies analysis: the poem which begins "My life had stood—a loaded gun," which I would like to read you.

> My life had stood—a Loaded Gun
> In Corners—till a Day
> The Owner passed—identified—
> And carried Me away—
>
> And now We roam in Sovreign Woods—
> And now We hunt the Doe—
> And every time I speak for Him—
> The Mountains straight reply—
>
> And do I smile, such cordial light
> Upon the Valley glow—
> It is as a Vesuvian face
> Had let its pleasure through—
>
> And when at Night—Our good Day done—
> I guard My Master's head—
> 'Tis better than the Eider-Duck's
> Deep Pillow—to have shared—
>
> To foe of His—I'm deadly foe—
> None stir the second time—
> On whom I lay a Yellow Eye—
> Or an emphatic Thumb—
>
> Though I than He—may longer live
> He longer must—than I—
> For I have but the power to kill,
> Without—the power to die—(754)

Is this an allegory, and if so of what? Is it a cry from some psychic deep where good and evil are not to be separated? In any case, it is a poem whose reverberations are infinite, as in great music; and we can only guess with what agony it was written down.

This power to say the unsayable—to hint of the unknowable—is the power of the seer, in this woman equipped with an ironic intelligence and great courage of spirit. The stuff of Emily Dickinson's imagination is of this world; there is nothing macabre about her material (in the manner of Poe) and there is very little of the labored or artificial about her means. If "she mastered life by rejecting it," she mastered that Nature concerning which she had such ambivalent feeling by adding herself to the sum of all things, in a Rilkean habit of praise. "She kept in touch with reality," someone has said of her, "by the clearest and finest of the senses—the sense of sight. Perhaps the great vitality of contact by vision is the essence, in part, of her originality." How exactly she renders the creatures of this earth! She gives them to us, not as symbols of this or that, but as themselves. And her lyrical notation is so precise, so fine and moves so closely in union with her mind, that she is continually striking out aphorisms, as is usual in mystical writing from Plotinus to Blake. And as her life goes on, everything becomes whittled down, evanescent. Her handwriting becomes a kind of fluid print; her poems become notations; all seems to be on the point of disappearing. And suddenly all disappears.

"She was a visionary," says Richard Chase, "to whom truth came with exclusive finality [and] like her Puritan forbears she was severe, downright, uncompromising, visionary, factual, sardonic."

"My business is to create," said the poet Blake. "My business is circumference," said the poet Dickinson. And we know that the physical center of that circumference was to remain the town of Amherst, which almost exactly one hundred years ago (on December 10th, 1859) Miss Dickinson described with great charm and deep affection, in a letter to Mrs. Samuel Bowles: "It storms in Amherst five days—it snows, and then it rains, and then soft fogs like vails hang on all the houses, and then the days turn Topaz, like a lady's pin . . ."—as delicate a description as a New England town and New England winter weather have ever received.

Words

by Charles R. Anderson

"For several years," wrote Emily Dickinson of the period just prior to her first great outburst of poetic creation, "my Lexicon—was my only companion." This ambiguous reply to Higginson's query about her friends led him to emphasize the wrong half of her meaning. He could only be touched by the pathos of her lonely life. The possibility would not have occurred to him that for the poet, as distinguished from the person, a dictionary could be far more valuable than society. As a woman she was well aware that deprivation in life might be one of the pressures that produced art. Referring to some crisis, either a loss through death or the denial of love's feast, she could describe the verbal substitute as a dry wine: "Easing my famine/At my Lexicon." But as a poet she knew that words were the only medium of her art, like colors to the painter and notes to the composer. They are the molds which give form to the thoughts and things of experience. Indeed, experience is without meaning until it finds its identity in words. She would have applauded Auden's quip: "How can I know what I think till I see what I say?" The reason we can never learn on earth to know each other, she wrote, is that only heaven can provide the vocabulary for that most buried secret, which puzzles us here "Without the lexicon." With it, words can become instruments of knowledge. A number of her poems are explicitly concerned with the power and the problems of language.

The declaration that during the crucial years her "Lexicon" was her only companion occurs in the context of a letter exclusively concerned with her intellectual and poetic development. Looked at from the standpoint of art rather than biography it takes on an importance that cannot be treated lightly, even though it should not be interpreted too literally. She thumbed unweariedly her great copy of Webster's *American Dictionary of the English Language* in the enlarged edition of 1847, referred to hereafter as her Lexicon. But she had other sources of language. One was the vocabulary in action she absorbed from her reading. She ranged

widely among books but selected with fine discrimination, as shown by
her characterization of those most useful to her.

Of some book, presumably the Bible, she said: "Should you ask me my
comprehension of a starlight Night, Awe were my only reply, and so of
the mighty Book—It stills, incites, infatuates—blesses and blames in
one. . . . A Word is inundation, when it comes from the Sea." Of the
dramatic poet whom she knew by heart: "While Shakespeare remains
Literature is firm." These were parts of the great Lexicon from which she
learned the way of words. The former was one of her chief sources of
imagery, the latter her chief model in revitalizing language through new
strategies. But her style was never Biblical or Shakespearean, as with
writers like Melville. Instead of surface borrowings she plundered them
outright, stealing the secrets by which they gave life and power to words,
but transvaluating them so as to create an idiom all her own.

From the Bible she learned, among other things, the mode of juxta-
posing elemental concrete things with equally fundamental ideas and
feelings—grass, stone, heart, majesty, despair. But this method of achieving universality is given novelty by reducing the Bible's expansive narra-
tive to startlingly compact lyrics. She rarely alludes to its stories and characters, except in the humorous poems, employing instead a subtler technique. Her stolen images, though sometimes overtly used, are normally
assimilated to her own style by being wrenched into unexpected contexts
(as when the cross becomes the block on which the "Auctioneer of Parting" brings his hammer down), or so submerged in her poems that only
long peering below the surface reveals their allusive richness (as in two
poems on the finding and losing of love, "Mine by the Royal *Seal*" and
"Faith *bleats* to understand"). When she actually borrows any of its
phrasings they are used as counters to be played against the rational
terminology of science, just as she maneuvered the trite and sentimental
against the iconoclastic. In fact, her battling with language is quite similar
to her skirmishes with the Bible, The Word, poking them both to make
them come alive. She had heard enough sermons and hymns to know how
inert these once great Scriptures could become in the hands of imitators,
The Bay Psalm Book being a grim reminder. Perhaps these were the
principal words on which she had been fed from childhood, and her
revolt against them as theology was paralleled by her revolt against the
language in which their doctrines were cast. In a sense, the Bible was the
divine adversary she must overcome by assimilation in order to utter her
own scriptures.

Her debt to Shakespeare was just as pervasive and even less visible.
Poetic language in mid-nineteenth-century America had been reduced to
a relatively flat and nerveless state, but he furnished her with clues for its
resurrection. The major writers of the preceding generation had not only
finished their careers but had brought the older way to a dead end. For a
poet to come of age at such a time, as she did, may have been a handicap

in that it deprived her of a living tradition within which or against which to work. But it also lessened the danger of derivativeness, such as had weighed so heavily on the writers following Milton, for example, and offered the advantage of challenge to original spirits. It would be interesting to inquire concerning such a bold experimenter with words whether her distinction does not derive from the very *élan* with which she drove forward out of the verbal doldrums in which she found herself. Shakespeare and the metaphysical poets wrought such miracles with language in the Renaissance, and Eliot and Pound took up a similar task in the twentieth century.

The devices all of them used to achieve "semantic rejuvenation," as pointed out recently by a distinguished linguist, sound like a summary of the techniques employed by a private New England poet in the 1860's. Etymology was one of them, sending the reader back to root meanings in order to force his participation in the esthetic experience. Here Dickinson is actually cited as a forerunner of modern poetic usage, but the other devices were part of her practice as well. Substitution of simple concrete terms for the abstract ones actually intended was her strategy for achieving vivid immediacy, and the opposite for giving transcendent value to the homely. Juxtaposition of words out of different connotative spheres she employed for ironic contrast, as with the legal and the amorous, and abrupt changes from one level of discourse to another for rhetorical shock, as from the serious to the comic, from eloquence to bald statement. Close kin to these are her rearrangements of word order to secure emphasis and surprise, deliberately rather than through ineptness, often merely by exaggerating a familiar colloquial usage.

All these she probably learned from her great master. Two final devices are more recognizably Shakespearean. One is the shifting of grammatical categories (for example, "pomp" as an adjective, "create" as a participle), by which she discovered forms that were both shortened and novel. This gives a slightly archaic flavor to her verse that has been objected to as affectation, but she would have justified her sparing use of it, like Hopkins, as one of the admissible special "graces" of the boldly original poet. The other is her exploitation of punning, after centuries of disrepute, not in a frivolous context but as the legitimate adjunct of a superbly serious style. In thanking a friend for a happy pun she once commented: "How lovely are the wiles of Words." No weighty pronouncement could express her kinship with the Elizabethans more effectively than this apparently casual remark.

When paying her ultimate tribute to Shakespeare she had asked, "Why is any other book needed?" but she did not mean this as abject surrender to the great figure that loomed for her out of the literary past. For her there was another book needed, one she was compelled to write, the volume of her own poems. To do this she felt she had to vanquish another giant by trying to draw the strength of his mighty sword to her pebble-sling. In suggesting how much she learned from this unequal battle, there is no intention of setting up false comparisons. It is enough to claim that her talent came to life by absorbing the revolutionary quality of her tradition in its most vital expression, without losing her individuality. So with the other books available to her. She searched them for what they had to offer and absorbed their lessons, but was never bookish. As a result, literary sources and analogues are the least fruitful approaches to her poetry. She simply acted on Emerson's maxim, "Imitation is suicide," without any theorizing about artistic integrity other than the quiet remark, "I . . . never consciously touch a paint, mixed by another person." If she ever went through any period of real apprenticeship to any of her masters, no compositions indicating it have survived.

Another source of her poetic language was the particular idiom of her heritage in the living speech of the Connecticut Valley. Some of her special linguistic techniques sprang from native roots, and she underscored the importance of this by making it the conscious theme of several poems. One of her devices for putting new life in the literary vocabulary was to employ a fair sprinkling of homely and dialectal expressions. Though deplored by earlier editors who tried to purge her text of them (changing "heft" to "weight," for example), it was deliberate, as proved by her defense of regionalism on general grounds as the truest mode of perception. So robin, nut, and winter in her poetry, "Because I see—New Englandly," she said, coining a wry adverb; had she been cuckoo born, she would sing like the British, for they too in their own way see "provincially." With none of the fanfare of professional literary nationalists like Whitman, she quietly set about exploring the poetic resources of the American language, including New England localisms, though she never limited herself to one vocabulary.

In Amherst she breathed an academic air as naturally as a rural one, and she adroitly played off the learned word against the simple Saxon for special effects in many poems. One illustration will make this clear. In contrasting the old-fashioned religious view with the newer one of science, she takes advantage of the historical composition of the English language, which has chiefly drawn from the classical tongues its speculative and technological words. The wit and irony of the following quatrain is wholly the result of this linguistic maneuvering:

> "Faith" is a fine invention
> When Gentlemen can *see*—
> But *Microscopes* are prudent
> In an Emergency.

The faith of the fathers is rendered in the native language, the modern doubt in foreign borrowings.

The deliberateness of this contrast is shown in the skill with which she

complicates the issues by throwing one unexpected Latinate word into
the first line, so that faith becomes a mechanical thing; New Englanders,
she is aware, had won fame as inventors, not only of things but of the
Puritan theocracy. More subtly, she chooses as the defining word for
microscopes that they are "prudent." This word means worldly wise, and
is associated in American history with Benjamin Franklin, the great
advocate of rational utility. But it also carried with it the medieval religious meaning of *prudens,* endowed with the capacity of perceiving divine
truth. One of the best of the early Christian poets took the pen name of
"Prudentius," and Puritan parents as well as clergy had kept the idea
alive by christening their daughters Prudence. Science, then, furnishes the
instrument for seeing God? The final irony is in the use of "Gentlemen,"
deriving from both Latin and Saxon sources, hardly the word Cotton
Mather would have used for the faithful. Does this suggest the decay of
religion in her own day to a social propriety? We are not told what they
see, nor what the "Emergency" is when they must resort to microscopes.
Any need for really seeing is an emergency, and in spiritual matters the
crisis was particularly acute during the last half of the nineteenth century.
The linguistic web is drawn tight, and the ambiguity heightened by
deftly compressing the whole conflict between religion and science into
sixteen words. But this is a word game, not a poem.

No child of the region ever exploited the laconic temperament so suc-
cessfully in poetry. In striking contrast with the practice of her contemporaries is the brevity of her own forms, which she celebrated in an
aphorism:

> Capacity to Terminate
> Is a Specific Grace—

This gift she developed into a highly elliptical style, pruning away all
excess in her passion to get down to the clean bones of language. In a
poem about writing a love letter the urgency of the message makes her
impatient of verbosity and even the standard rules of construction:

> Tell Him—I only said the Syntax—
> And left the Verb and the pronoun out—

The lines also describe her own poetic way.

Another technique, thought of as peculiarly Dickinsonian, is of course
the way of all poetry—by indirection. But the oblique approach, the
sudden and unexpected turn, becomes such a pervasive habit as to constitute her unique mode of expression. "Tell all the Truth but tell it
slant," she says, for it must be perceived and revealed gradually or it will
dazzle into blindness. A passage in Emerson's "Uriel" may have suggested
the metaphor by which she justifies the circuitous approach:

> Too bright for our infirm Delight
> The Truth's superb surprise.

Slant and surprise, the distinctive marks of her best poetry, are the result of her brilliant verbal strategy. A kinship, rather than an influence, is revealed by the analogies that can be drawn from Emerson's *Poems*, one of her most cherished possessions being the copy given her in 1850 by the friend who first awakened her mind and creative powers. There she could have read, in "Merlin" the archetypal poet, the best possible epigraph for her own poetic achievement:

> He shall aye climb
> For his rhyme. . . .
> But mount to paradise
> By the stairway of surprise.

Concerned with expression from her earliest years, she is clearly referring to her need for freedom in finding her own voice when she complains in one of her poems: "They shut me up in Prose." "They" were all the forces that militated against her being a poet. Living in a family of practical people and in an isolated community, she had little encouragement to leave the common-sense ways of prose. What she said of her father in a letter of 1851 could be applied to her environment as a whole, that he was too intent on "real life" to have any interest in poetry. Similarly, at about the same time, she wrote to one of her few companions in wit and literature: "[We] please ourselves with the fancy that we are the only poets, and everyone else is *prose*." Prose to her was limited, as the similes in the poem put it, like being shut up in a closet when a girl so she would be "still," or like putting a bird in prison. If they had only peeped and seen her "brain go round," she says, they would have known she had the madness of a poet who would not stay shut up in convention. The true singer breaks out of any prison, as the bird by an effort of will abolishes his captivity and sings. So she too, even in the letters which were virtually her only medium of expression until about the age of twenty-eight, broke out of the narrow limits of prose into poetic freedoms that make it hard to draw a line between her use of the two modes. "They shut me up in Prose" may also refer to the conventional kind of verse her mentors urged upon her when she finally did venture into poetry. For this poem was written at the very end of 1862, after that first remarkable exchange with Higginson, the only letters in which they seriously discussed artistic problems. She soon put him down as another of those who would shut her up in prose, whom she must escape if she wanted to mount the stairway of surprise. . . .

The Private World:
Poems of Emily Dickinson

by Archibald MacLeish

. . . Having by now raised more vexed questions about poetry than a
modest book ought decently to contain, and having settled them, if at all,
only as one might settle a roomful of difficult visitors in an uneasy watching circle, I turn, for my remaining four chapters, to the particulars of
poetry itself, which is to say, to the poems of four quite different poets.
But I turn to them not to write essays on these poets: I would not know
how to expatiate "on" any one of the four—and certainly not in such
brief compass. Rather, I wish to use their poems to continue in terms of
ends the examination of the means of poetry to which the foregoing
chapters have been devoted. In those earlier chapters I attempted to
discuss the means to meaning which the art of poetry employs—that
relating of the unrelated which seems to reveal the *analogie universelle*
by which, as poets say, their art gives reasons to experience. In these
chapters I wish to examine, not the means to meaning, but meanings
themselves as specific poems have discerned them in specific experiences:
the experience of the private world; the experience of the public world;
the experience of the rejection of the world; the experience of the acceptance of the world.

However, I must admit at the outset that it is not possible wholly to
separate means from meaning in poetry or in any other art, for the means
contain the meaning. Emily Dickinson is an obvious example precisely
because her poems appear to prove the contrary. On first reading there
are no means; there is nothing but meaning. Her use of words as sounds
is simple—as simple as the hymnbook from which she borrowed it. Her
organization of words as meanings, though sometimes a little difficult, a
little too colloquial or not quite colloquial enough, appears to be de-
cipherable in the usual way of prose. Her images are so familiar as to be
barely visible or so strangely abstracted as to be almost transparent. And
her reader, her first-time reader, often ends, not with a handful of poems,

but with a handful of aphorisms such as: good comes from evil, having is
taught by having not, suffering enriches. It is only by a second reading—
or by another reader—that the aphorisms can be turned back into poems
and discovered to mean something very different. And this rereading involves, of course, a reconsideration of those means to meaning—an opening of eyes and ears.

One can begin with the ears. It is true that the patterns of Emily's
sounds are simple, both rhythmically and otherwise.

> Our share of night to bear—
> Our share of morning—
> Our blank in bliss to fill
> Our blank in scorning—
>
> Here a star, and there a star,
> Some lose their way!
> Here a mist, and there a mist,
> Afterwards—Day!   (113)

The second stanza varies the pattern established by the first but the
pattern of the first is as persistent and graceless as that of any common
hymn. But though the same thing is true of the sound of many—perhaps
most—of Emily's poems, something else is true also. A protracted reading
may set a metronome to ticking in the ear but a protracted reading will
also demonstrate that the simplicity and even the gracelessness of the
structure of sound has something to do with the power of the poem to
contain what it contains. Few poets, Blake among them, have used words
as sounds in as primitive a way while using the same words as meanings
in a way so far from primitive. And not even Blake pushed his organization of words as meanings as far toward the unsayable as Emily sometimes
did in these simple-sounding little tunes:

> A solemn thing—it was—I said—
> A Woman—white—to be—
> And wear—if God should count me fit—
> Her blameless mystery—
>
> A timid thing—to drop a life
> Into the mystic well—
> Too plummetless—that it come back—
> Eternity—until—   (271)

What becomes obvious on careful reading, in other words, is the fact that
Emily, far from ignoring the structure of words as sounds, employs it
deliberately and consciously to hold, in firm shapes of emphatic rhythm,
structures of words as meanings which, without such firm support, might

have disintegrated into meaninglessness. It is not syntax, you will have noticed, which holds the end of that last poem together: ". . . that it come back—/Eternity—until—"

No, I know no poems in which the double structure of words as sounds and words as meanings—that curious relationship of the logically unrelated—will be found, on right reading, to be more *comprehensive* than it is in the poems of Emily Dickinson. But the same thing is not true of the coupling of Emily's images, either in metaphor or out of it. Here it takes more than a second reading or even a third to demonstrate that there are images at work at all. "Amethyst remembrance," "Polar expiation." Neither of these exists upon the retina. Neither can be brought into focus by the muscles of the eye. The "blue and gold mistake" of Indian summer seems to exist somewhere in the visible—or would if one could only get rid of that "mistake." And so too does "The Distance/On the look of Death" and ". . . Dying—is a different way—/ A Kind behind the Door." But who can describe the graphic shape of ". . . that white sustenance/Despair"? And yet all of these present themselves as images, do they not?—*act* as images? Where can remembrance be amethyst? Where but in the eye?

The difficulty, I think, has a double cause. First, the "objects" of Emily's images are often not objects at all but abstractions used as though they were objects—abstractions presented for the eye to see and the ear to hear and the hand to touch. Second, the objects, when they are objects, are often "transparent" in the manner of the visible member of that coupling we call a symbol.

> At Half past Three, a single Bird
> Unto a silent Sky
> Propounded but a single term
> Of cautious melody.
>
> At Half past Four, Experiment
> Had subjugated test
> And lo, Her silver Principle
> Supplanted all the rest.
>
> At Half past Seven, Element
> Nor Implement, be seen—
> And Place was where the Presence was
> Circumference between.   (1084)

Here at the beginning, before dawn, there is a bird audible to the ear as a true bird should be—a "single term" under "a silent Sky." An hour later, the full song has supplanted the tentative beginning but has become "silver Principle" in the process. And by half past seven the song is over both as the "Element" it had been first and the "Implement" it had become later, while, as for the bird that sang, it has turned itself into a "Presence" beyond "Circumference." And besides it has vanished: in its stead there is only "Place"—the visible world of daylight well this side of "Circumference."

Richard Wilbur has a marvelous saying about this translucence of Emily's "objects": ". . . what mortal objects she does acknowledge are riddled by desire to the point of transparency." And this is true, though it is not always true. She can catch that most uncatchable of all God's creatures, the hummingbird, in an image as firm and impervious as a figure in enamel: "Within my Garden rides a Bird/Upon a single Wheel." And she can go on to complete the figure in a miraculous design of words which captures the bird not as bird but as tumble of blossoms and resonance of color:

> A Route of Evanescence
> With a revolving Wheel—
> A Resonance of Emerald—
> A Rush of Cochineal—
> And every Blossom on the Bush
> Adjusts it's tumbled Head—
> The mail from Tunis, probably,
> An easy Morning's Ride—   (1463)

But such images as these are rare. The more characteristic image lets the light through either by pushing the natural object back until it seems to become an abstraction, or by drawing the abstraction forward until it has the look or feel of an object ("that white sustenance/Despair"), or by doing both together in a coupling of the two. And it is here, of course, that the difficulty resolves itself. For the moment it becomes apparent that Emily is using objects and abstractions in this inverted and inverting fashion, it becomes apparent that images *are* in constant play and that their coupling is a coupling back and forth, not only between incongruities, but between worlds—the visible and the invisible.

How does she accomplish her metamorphoses? How does she turn abstraction like Grace and Bliss and Balm and Crown and Peninsula and Circumference—the most abstract of abstractions and capitalized as well—into sensual counterweights that feel in the hand like images even if they can't be seen? The poems of almost any other poet would go down, founder, if they put to sea in generalizations as leaky as these, but Emily uses them over and over and a dozen others besides (Morn, Noon, Earl, Pod, Plush, Eden) and never ships a drop. How does she manage it? By the tone, I think, in which she speaks them—by the voice in which she makes you hear. *Decalogue* is one of her words and written with a capital D to leave no question that she means the Ten Commandments. But listen to her use of it in this poem:

> To make One's Toilette—after Death
> Has made the Toilette cool
> Of only Taste we cared to please
> Is difficult, and still—
>
> That's easier—than Braid the Hair—
> And make the Boddice gay—
> When eyes that fondled it are wrenched
> By Decalogues—away—   (485)

You see, of course, what is being said. To make one's toilet when the only taste we cared to please has disappeared in death is difficult but even that is easier than braiding the hair and making the bodice gay "When eyes that fondled it are wrenched/By Decalogues—away." There is nothing abstract or generalized about *those* Ten Commandments. The word has been changed in saying it—changed in the voice that says. Not only has the poem a *voice* (not all poems do) but it has a particular voice—Emily's voice. And it is by reason of that particularity that these universalizations of Emily's are changed to "things." Universal words enunciated by a universal voice are not poetry. They are not even interesting. (Or perhaps I should not say "even": "En art," as LaForgue observed, "il s'agit d'être interessant.") But universal words, generalizations, abstractions, made particular in a particular voice can be poetry. As Emily Dickinson proved once for all.

Tone is always important in any true poem: it is ignored at the reader's peril. But in poems such as Emily Dickinson's it is more than important: it is crucial. One of my students, speaking of one of Emily's most characteristic poems, insisted that it was made only of tone. He was wrong in fact but right in instinct, for without the particular tone he had noticed the poem could not have been written. And the same thing is true of almost all the poems which are most her own, most intimately hers. The reason is not obscure. When a poet commits himself to the private world, to his own private inward world, to the world of his own emotions, his own glimpses, his own delights and dreads and fearful hopes and hopeless despairs, his *voice,* the voice in which he speaks of what he sees and hears and touches in that near and yet far distant country, is more pervasive of his poems and more important to their meaning than the voice in poems from the public world or the world in nature or any other world "outside." The poet of the private world is not observer only but *actor* in the scene that he observes. And the voice that speaks in his poems is the voice of himself as actor—as sufferer of those sufferings, delighter in those delights—as well as his voice as poet. If the tone is false, if the voice is self-conscious, the poem becomes unbearable as well as bad; for the *actor* is then false, self-conscious. If the voice is dead, the poem is dead.

This was Emily's situation. Those of us who know a little of her life—and there is little any of us can know for it was a life in which little "happened"—those of us who know a little of her life are tempted to think of her as shut out: shut out from love; shut out from fame . . . a small, plain, spinster in a narrow village whom the world and everything else passed by. And it is true, of course, that she was a spinster and small and plain—though no one can really believe it who remembers what she said of the color of her own eyes—"like the sherry the guest leaves in the glass." It is true, too, that she left Amherst rarely—to go to South Hadley to school, to go to Boston several times when here eyes were troublesome, to go to Washington once when her father was a congressman and to stop at Philadelphia on the way back. But it is not true that her withdrawal into her father's house and into her own room in that house was a retreat from life. On the contrary it was an adventure into life—a penetration of the life she had elected to discover and explore—the vast and dangerous and often painful but always real—poignantly real—realer than any other—life of herself. Her business, she said, was circumference and circumference was the limit of experience, of her experience—the limit beyond which, you remember, that dawn bird disappeared when it turned Presence. Deprived of love? Perhaps she was as the world speaks of that deprivation, but no one can read her poems without learning that she knew more of love than most of us—knew more of what is *to* love. Deprived of fame? Perhaps. Hundreds and hundreds of little poems of which no one in Amherst knew—no one even in her father's house—over seventeen hundred in all—dropped into a box to be discovered when she died. But does any one really believe that the woman who wrote this poem knew nothing of fame?

> Lay this Laurel on the One
> Too intrinsic for Renown—
> Laurel—vail your deathless tree—
> Him you chasten, that is He!   (1393)

"Him you chasten," "He" who is deprived of fame, is probably her father, for the poem seems to have been written on the third anniversary of his death. But it was Emily who had learned that one can be "Too intrinsic for renown." Learning that, she had learned more truth about fame than most of those who think they possess it ever guess.

The miracle of that little poem lies, I think, in the word "intrinsic" and in the tone which makes that last line resonant with restraint and triumphant in revelation: "Him you chasten, that is He." Emily does not always reach that height but the tone rarely fails her. Hers is a New England voice—a voice which belongs to a woman who, as she said, "sees New Englandly." It has the New England respect for others which stands, at bottom, upon a respect for self. There is a poem of Emily's which none of us can read unmoved—which moves me, I confess, so deeply that I cannot always read it. It is a poem which, in another voice, might have cried aloud, but in hers is quiet. I think it is the quietness which moves me most. It begins with these six lines:

> I can wade Grief—
> Whole Pools of it—
> I'm used to that—
> But the least push of Joy
> Breaks up my feet—
> And I tip—drunken—   (252)

One has only to consider what this might have been, written otherwise by another hand—for it would have had to be another hand. Why is it not maudlin with self-pity here? Why does it truly touch the heart and the more the more it is read? Because it is impersonal? It could scarcely be more personal. Because it is oblique?—ironic? It is as candid as agony itself. No, because there *is* no self-pity. Because the tone which can contain "But the least push of Joy/Breaks up my feet . . ." is incapable of self-pity. When we drown in self-pity we throw ourselves into ourselves and go down. But the writer of this poem is both in it and out of it: both suffers it and sees.

There is another famous poem which makes the same point:

> She bore it till the simple veins
> Traced azure on her hand—
> Till pleading, round her quiet eyes
> The purple Crayons stand.
>
> Till Daffodils had come and gone
> I cannot tell the sum,
> And then she ceased to bear it—
> And with the Saints sat down . . .   (144)

Here again, as so often in her poems of death—and death is, of course, her familiar theme—the margin between mawkishness and emotion is thin, so thin that another woman, living as she lived in constant contemplation of herself, might easily have stumbled through. What saves her, and saves the poem, is the tone: "She bore it till . . ." "And then she ceased to bear it—/And with the Saints sat down." If you have shaped your mouth to say "And with the Saints sat down" you cannot very well weep for yourself or for anyone else, veins azure on the hand or not.

Anyone who will read Emily's poems straight through in their chronological order in Thomas H. Johnson's magnificent Harvard edition will feel, I think, as I do, that without her extraordinary mastery of tone her achievement would have been impossible. To write constantly of death, of grief, of despair, of agony, of fear is almost to insure the failure of art, for these emotions overwhelm the mind, and art must surmount experience to master it. A morbid art is an imperfect art. Poets must learn Yeats's lesson that life is tragedy but if the tragedy turns tragic for them they will be crippled poets. Like the ancient Chinese in "Lapis Lazuli" (or like our own beloved Robert Frost who has looked as long and deeply into the darkness of the world as a man well can), "their eyes, their ancient glittering eyes" must be *gay*. Emily's eyes, color of the sherry the guests leave in the glass, had that light in them:

> Dust is the only Secret—
> Death, the only One
> You cannot find out all about
> In his "native town."
>
> Nobody knew "his Father"—
> Never was a Boy—
> Had'nt any playmates,
> Or "Early history"—
>
> Industrious! Laconic!
> Punctual! Sedate!
> Bold as a Brigand!
> Stiller than a Fleet!
>
> Builds, like a Bird, too!
> Christ robs the Nest—
> Robin after Robin
> Smuggled to Rest!   (153)

Ezra Pound, in his translation of *The Women of Trachis*, has used a curiously compounded colloquialism which depends on just such locutions to make the long agony of Herakles supportable. Emily had learned the secret almost a century before.

But it is not only agony she is able to put in a supportable light by her mastery of tone. She can do the same thing with those two opposing subjects which betray so many poets: herself and God. She sees herself as small and lost and doubtless doomed—but sees herself always, or almost always, with a saving smile which is not entirely tender:

> Two full Autumns for the Squirrel
> Bounteous prepared—
> Nature, Had'st thou not a Berry
> For thy wandering Bird?   (846)

and

> A Drunkard cannot meet a Cork
> Without a Revery—
> And so encountering a Fly
> This January Day
> Jamaicas of Remembrance stir
> That send me reeling in—
> The moderate drinker of Delight
> Does not deserve the spring . . .   (1628)

I suppose there was never a more delicate dancing on the crumbling edge of the abyss of self-pity—that suicidal temptation of the lonely—than Emily's, but she rarely tumbles in. She sees herself in the awkward stumbling attitude and laughs.

As she laughs too, but with a child's air of innocence, at her father's Puritan God, that Neighbor over the fence of the next life in the hymnal:

> Abraham to kill him
> Was distinctly told—
> Isaac was an Urchin—
> Abraham was old—
>
> Not a hesitation—
> Abraham complied—
> Flattered by Obeisance
> Tyranny demurred—
>
> Isaac—to his children
> Lived to tell the tale—
> Moral—with a Mastiff
> Manners may prevail.   (1317)

It is a little mocking sermon which would undoubtedly have shocked Edward Dickinson with his "pure and terrible" heart, but it brings the god of Abraham closer to New England than He had been for the two centuries preceding—brings Him, indeed, as close as that growling watch-

dog in the next yard: so close that He can be addressed politely by the
child who always walked with Emily hand in hand:

> Lightly stepped a yellow star
> To it's lofty place
> Loosed the Moon her silver hat
> From her lustral Face
> All of Evening softly lit
> As an Astral Hall
> Father I observed to Heaven
> You are punctual—   (1672)

But more revealing than the confiding smile which makes it possible to
speak familiarly to the God of Elder Brewster is the hot and fearless
and wholly human anger with which she is able to face him at the end.
Other poets have confronted God in anger but few have been able to
manage it without rhetoric and posture. There is something about that
ultimate face to face which excites an embarrassing self-consciousness
in which the smaller of the two opponents seems to strut and "bear it
out even to the edge of doom." Not so with Emily. She speaks with the
laconic restraint appropriate to her country, which is New England, and
to herself, which is a small, shy gentlewoman who has suffered much:

> Of God we ask one favor,
> That we may be forgiven—
> For what, he is presumed to know—
> The Crime, from us, is hidden—
> Immured the whole of Life
> Within a magic Prison . . .   (1601)

It is a remarkable poem and its power, indeed its possibility, lies almost
altogether in its voice, its tone. The figure of the magic prison is beautiful in itself, but it is effective in the poem because of the level at which
the poem is spoken—the level established by that "he is presumed to
know." At another level even the magic prison might well become pre-
tentious.

But what then is this tone? How does this unforgettable voice speak
to us? For one thing, and most obviously, it is a wholly spontaneous
tone. There is no literary assumption of posture or pose in advance.
There is no sense that a subject has been chosen—that a theme is about
to be developed. Occasionally, in the nature pieces, the sunset scenes,
which are so numerous in the early poems, one feels the presence of
the pad of water-color paper and the mixing of the tints, but when she
began to write as poet, which she did, miraculously, within a few months

of her beginnings as a writer, all that awkwardness disappears. Breath is drawn and there are words that will not leave you time to watch her coming toward you. Poem after poem—more than a hundred and fifty of them—begin with the word "I," the talker's word. She is already in the poem before she begins it, as a child is already in the adventure before he finds a word to speak of it. To put it in other terms, few poets and they among the most valued—Donne comes again to mind—have written more *dramatically* than Emily Dickinson, more in the live locutions of dramatic speech, words born living on the tongue, written as though spoken. Few have committed themselves as actors more livingly to the scene. It is almost impossible to begin one of her successful poems without finishing it. The punctuation may bewilder you. The density of the thing said may defeat your understanding. But you will read on nevertheless because you will not be able to stop reading. Something is being said to you and you have no choice but hear.

And this is a second characteristic of that voice—that it not only *speaks* but speaks to *you*. We are accustomed in our time—unhappily accustomed, I think—to the poetry of the overheard soliloquy, the poetry written by the poet to himself or to a little group of the like-minded who can be counted on in advance to "understand." Poetry of this kind can discover worlds when the poet is Rilke but even in Rilke there is something sealed and unventilated about the discovery which sooner or later stifles the birds. The subject of all poetry is the human experience and its object must therefore be humanity as well, even in a time like ours when humanity seems to prefer to limit its knowledge of the experience of life to the life the advertisers offer it. It is no excuse to a poet that humanity will not listen. It never has listened unless it was made to.

Emily knew that as well as we do. The materialism and vulgarity of those years after the Civil War when she reached her maturity as an artist may not have been as flagrant as the materialism and vulgarity in which we live but the parochialism was even greater. America was immeasurably farther from Europe, where the arts were at least domesticated, and Amherst was farther from the rest of America, and in and about Amherst there was no one near enough to see the poems she was writing except for the occasional verse sent across the lawn to her brother's wife or mailed to Colonel Higginson in Boston or to her father's friend, the editor of the *Springfield Republican,* or shown to her sister Lavinia. But her poems, notwithstanding, were never written to herself. The voice one hears in them is never a voice *overheard.* On the contrary, it is a voice which speaks to us, strangers—and how strange we would have seemed to Emily Dickinson!—so urgently, so immediately, so *individually,* that most of us are half in love with this dead girl we all call by her first name, and read with indignation Colonel Higginson's account of her as "a plain, shy little person . . . without a single good feature."

It is this liveness in the voice that makes the curious history of Emily's poems more curious. I know no greater paradox in the whole paradoxical account of the preservation of manuscripts than Emily Dickinson's commitment of that live voice of hers to a private box full of snippets of paper—old bills, invitations to commencements, clippings from newspapers—tied together with little loops of thread. Other poets have published to the world verses which, we think, should have been delivered privately to the three or four in a position to decipher the postmark. Emily locked away in a chest a voice which speaks to every living creature of the things which every living creature knows. . . .

Emily Dickinson's Prose

by David J. M. Higgins

> An earnest letter is or should be a life-warrant or death-warrant, for what
> is each instant but a gun, harmless because "unloaded," but that touched
> "goes off?"
>
> —Emily Dickinson

"Last night the Warings had their novel wedding festival." T. W.
Higginson wrote to his sister in 1876. "The Woolseys were bright as
usual & wrote some funny things for different guests—one imaginary
letter to me from my partially cracked poetess at Amherst, who writes
to me & signs 'Your scholar'" (II, 570).[1]

The partially cracked poetess, Emily Dickinson, had no idea her letters
were shown to strangers or parodied, but she knew they were unusual.
A few days before Higginson enjoyed the Woolseys' imitation of her
style, Emily had sent his wife Emerson's *Representative Men* as "a little
Granite Book you can lean upon." In lieu of a signature she had written,
"I am whom you infer—" (II, 569).

Mrs. Higginson had no trouble inferring. The prose of Emily Dickinson was as unmistakable as her poetry. In both she tried to condense
thought to its essence in epigram, trusting her reader to solve the puzzling paradoxes and puns and ambiguities along the way. While her
contemporaries gushed pages of nature description, Emily achieved single sentences like "The lawn is full of south and the odors tangle, and
I hear today for the first the river in the tree" (II, 452). Such impression-
ism, for all its economy and beauty, must have sounded strange to mid-
Victorian ears. Prose, especially in letters, was supposed to be prosaic.

"Emily Dickinson's Prose." From *Portrait of Emily Dickinson: The Poet and Her
Prose* (Unpublishd doctoral dissertation, Columbia University, 1961) by David J. M.
Higgins. Copyright © 1961 by David J. M. Higgins. Reprinted by permission of
David J. M. Higgins.

[1] Thomas H. Johnson and Theodora V. W. Ward, eds., *The Letters of Emily Dickinson* (Cambridge, Mass.: The Belknap Press of Harvard University Press, 1958), II, 570.
References to this edition (hereafter called *Letters*) will be indicated in the text by
volume and page number only, in parentheses.

Emily was aware of this: about 1865 she parodied the flatness of most correspondence by writing a poem in the form of a letter:

> Bee! I'm expecting you!
> Was saying Yesterday
> To Somebody you know
> That you were due—
>
> The Frogs got Home last Week—
> Are settled, and at work—
> Birds, mostly back—
> The Clover warm and thick—
>
> You'll get my Letter by
> The seventeenth; Reply
> Or better, be with me—
> Yours, Fly.[2]

If Emily Dickinson's letters did not sound like Fly's, it was because the subtlety and surprise of her thoughts required subtle and surprising words.

A biographical portrait of Emily Dickinson is necessarily the portrait of a letter-writer. Emily's physical existence in the Dickinson homestead was merely a round of household chores, aside from her writing. Her poems, except for those sent to friends as messages, are doubtful sources of fact. There are few accounts of her conversation because she preferred to write to her friends rather than see them. Indeed, some of her most intimate friendships were conducted almost entirely by mail. When, in her early thirties, she decided against publishing her poems, letters became the sole vehicles for her poetry. Her eventual publication and her present rank as a world poet depend to a great extent on the letters she wrote to Colonel Higginson and Mabel Loomis Todd, her posthumous editors. Higginson visited Emily only twice; Mrs. Todd talked with her between rooms and around corners but never met her face to face.

It is not a great exaggeration, then, to say that Emily Dickinson lived through the mail. Such a life is a hindrance to biography: the usual travels, public appearances, meetings with other poets, cricitism by contemporaries, and so on, all are lacking. On the other hand, her very remoteness from her neighbors gives her posthumous audience an advantage. Today's reader of Emily's letters can know her almost as well as the friends who received the letters nearly a century ago. In fact, the modern

---

[2] Thomas H. Johnson, ed. *The Poems of Emily Dickinson* (Cambridge: The Belknap Press of Harvard University Press, 1955), II, 734-35. This edition hereafter will be referred to as *Poems*.

reader may know her better than the correspondents who neither met her nor had access to her letters to others. For Emily Dickinson was audience-conscious; she carefully adapted each correspondence to her estimate of the reader's capacities. Today it is possible to compare letters and to see that Emily sent her most prosaic messages to dull friends, her most striking, oblique flashes of thought to those who would grasp them.

Sometimes she misjudged. She thought Helen Hunt Jackson, for instance, acute enough to understand the most esoteric letters. Though Mrs. Jackson was the only contemporary to call Emily Dickinson a great poet, she could not measure up to Emily's pronouncement, "Helen of Troy will die, but Helen of Colorado, never" (III, 889). In October 1875 Emily sent the following wedding congratulation to Helen Jackson:

> Have I a word but Joy?
>
> E. Dickinson.
> Who fleeing from the Spring
> The Spring avenging fling
> To Dooms of Balm—
>
> (II, 544)

Mrs. Jackson returned the note, asking for an explanation. Emily did not reply, of course. To do so would have been like explaining a joke.

Whatever the disadvantages of society-by-mail, there were rewards as well. Emily Dickinson lived deliberately and preferred to present herself to the world only by deliberate art. On the rare occasions when Emily met her friends, she made almost theatrical entrances, dressed completely in white and carrying flowers. Her conversations at such times are said to have been brilliant, but a conversation can have no second draft. Letters, however, can be deliberate creations from salutation to signature, and the letters of Emily Dickinson show a great deal of "stage presence."

Emily's creation of a letter might begin years before she mailed the final draft. Among her papers at the time of her death were hundreds of scraps and drafts of her writing. Some were torn corners of envelopes or backs of grocery lists; others were fair copies ready for mailing, or letters marred by corrections. The collection included poetry and prose in all stages of composition. It was the scrapbasket of Emily's workshop and she kept it as other New England women saved string and wrapping paper and ribbon, against a future need.

The greater part of the scrapbasket collection is poetry, but there is much prose, almost entirely in the handwriting of Emily's last ten years, 1876-86. Certainly she made earlier collections: phrases and whole sentences were repeated in letters written years apart. Probably she systematically destroyed all but the last group.

Emily jotted sentences as they occurred to her while she worked in the kitchen or garden. The roughest of the scraps were penciled scrawls, almost illegible, on any handy bit of paper. Later, in her room, she added them to her workshop collection. When she wrote letters she chose appropriate fragments and worked them into her prose. Sometimes the letter as a whole would pass through two or more drafts before it satisfied her. Meantime she would have chosen poems from the scrap-basket or from her "packets" [3] and fitted them also into her letter. The final writing—the letter her correspondent actually received—might look spontaneous, but it was the last of several creative stages.

An illustration of Emily's method of composition is a letter of 1885 to Helen Hunt Jackson. The message Emily mailed is missing, but all the preliminary drafts remain. On February 3, 1885, Mrs. Jackson wrote to Emily from California. She described her convalescence from a badly broken leg, and the natural beauty of Santa Monica:

> —As I write—(in bed, before breakfast,) I am looking straight off toward Japan—over a silver sea—my foreground is a strip of high grass, and mallows, with a row of Eucalyptus trees sixty or seventy feet high:—and there is a positive cackle of linnets.
>
> Searching, here, for Indian relics, especially the mortars or bowls hollowed out of stone, . . . I have found two Mexican women called *Ramona*, from whom I have bought the Indian mortars.—
>
> I hope you are well—and at work—I wish I knew what your portfolios, by this time, hold.
>
> (III, 869)

The "portfolios" Mrs. Jackson wondered about contained, among other things, the following prose fragments: "Strength to perish is sometimes withheld" and "Afternoon and the West and the gorgeous nothings which compose the sunset keep their high Appointment Clogged only with Music like the Wheels of Birds" (III, 868). The final phrase appeared in another fragment somewhat altered: "It is very still in the world now—Thronged only with Music like the Decks of Birds and the Seasons take their hushed places like figures in a Dream—" (III, 868).

Early in March, Emily composed her reply to Mrs. Jackson. Her first draft included the first two fragments, as well as a poem which Emily had used in a letter to Eben J. Loomis the previous January:

> Dear friend—
> To reproach my own Foot in behalf of your's, is involuntary, and finding myself, no solace in "whom he loveth he chasteneth" your Valor astounds

[3] "Packet" does not accurately describe the booklet grouping into which Emily Dickinson gathered hundreds of poems. Each booklet is made up of several sheets of paper, lightly sewn together along the left margin. I use the word "packet" because it is used throughout *Poems*. Emily Dickinson's word for the booklets is not known; Lavinia Dickinson called them "volumes," Millicent Todd Bingham, "fascicles."

me. It was only a small Wasp, said the French physician, repairing the sting, but the strength to perish is sometimes withheld, though who but you could tell a Foot.

> Take all away from me, but leave me Ecstasy
> And I am richer then, than all my Fellow Men.

> Is it becoming me to dwell so wealthily
> When at my very Door are those possessing more,
> In abject poverty?

That you compass "Japan" before you breakfast, not in the least surprises me, clogged only with the Music, like the Wheels of Birds.

Thank you for hoping I am well. Who could be ill in March, that Month of proclamation? Sleigh Bells and Jays contend in my Matinee, and the North surrenders, instead of the South, a reverse of Bugles.

Pity me, however, I have finished Ramona.

Would that like Shakespere, it were just published! Knew I how to pray, to intercede for your Foot were intuitive—but I am but a Pagan.

> Of God we ask one favor,
> That we may be forgiven—

(III, 866)

At this point the draft ends. The second draft continues to the end of the poem, adding, "May I know once more, and that you are saved?" It is signed, "Your Dickinson."

The greater part of the letter, answering Mrs. Jackson's, occurred to Emily as she wrote her first draft. The changes from one draft to the next are minor, but they are an artist's changes. The separate origin of the prose fragments seems to have caused most difficulty. Emily was dissatisfied with the words which introduced "Take all away from me. . . ." She cut out portions of the second draft and rearranged them, in effect creating a third draft. "But the strength to perish is sometimes withheld" finally became a separate sentence at the end of the poem. The second fragment was replaced by the third, its alternate form: "That you glance at Japan as you breakfast, not in the least surprises me, thronged only with Music, like the Decks of Birds" (III, 867).

Emily's fragmentary prose could serve more than one purpose. Another 1885 letter adapts the last quoted scrap to the memory of Judge Otis Lord: "He did not tell me he 'sang' to you, though to sing in his presence was involuntary, thronged only with Music, like the Decks of Birds" (III, 861).

The exact point at which Emily Dickinson became conscious of prose style remains obscure, but it certainly was early. In the first months of 1850, when she was nineteen, she wrote several letters in an exaggerated rhetoric which was nearly metrical. To her uncle Joel Norcross, who had failed to write to her after promising to do so, Emily depicted a light-hearted apocalyptic vision:

And I dreamed—and beheld a company whom no man may number—all men in their youth—all strong and stout-hearted—nor feeling their burdens for strength—nor waxing faint—nor weary. Some tended their flocks—and some sailed on the sea—and yet others kept gay stores, and deceived the foolish who came to buy. They made life one summer day—they danced to the sound of the lute—they sang old snatches of song—and they quaffed the rosy wine—One promised to love his friend and one vowed to defraud no poor—and *one* man told a lie to his niece—they all did sinfully—and their lives were not yet taken.

The letter went on to picture the forgetful uncle in hell and to deliver a series of curses: "You villain without rival—unparraleled [sic] doer of crimes—scoundrel unheard of before—disturber of public peace—'creation's blot and blank'—state's prison filler—*magnum bonum* promise maker—harum scarum promise breaker—" (I. 78). The final rhyme undoubtedly was intentional. A valentine letter of the following month, published in the Amherst College *Indicator* (and incidentally the only prose of Emily Dickinson known to have been published in her lifetime) contains three pieces of verse written as prose. The longest, with its typically Dickinsonian off-rhymes, can be read as four long lines or eight short ones: "Our friendship sir, shall endure till sun and moon shall wane no more, till stars shall set, and victims rise to grace the final sacrifice" (I, 92).

The first hints of Emily's later prose came in letters of 1854 to an Amherst College student, Henry Vaughan Emmons. Among the long-winded sentimental letters Emily was writing to others appear messages like this:

> Friend.
> I look in my casket and miss a pearl—I fear you intend to defraud me.
> Please not forget your promise to pay "mine own, with usury."
> I thank you for Hypatia, and ask you what it means?
>
> (I, 294)

Emily exchanged poems with Emmons and they discussed books. The tone of her letters to him became the one she adopted when writing to men of letters—especially Thomas Wentworth Higginson—a few years later. Eventually it spread to almost all her correspondence.

Letters of the mid-'fifties suggest the existence of a prose scrapbasket. In January 1855 Emily wrote to her brother's fiancée Susan Gilbert, "I fall asleep in tears, for your dear face, yet not one word comes back to me from that silent West. If it is finished, tell me, and I will raise the lid to my box of Phantoms, and lay one more love in . . ." (II, 315). The next year Emily used the final sentence again, altering it to fit the

departure of her cousin John Graves: "Ah John—*Gone?* Then I lift the
lid to my box of Phantoms, and lay another in, unto the Resurrection—"
(II, 330). In 1859 she wrote to Mrs. Joseph Haven, "Thank you for
recollecting me in the sweet moss—which with your memory, I have
lain in a little box, unto the Resurrection" (II, 357).

During the 1860's Emily seems to have repeated herself very little.
Perhaps she was more inventive than before or after; more likely,
though, she was conducting her correspondences so individually that few
sentences appropriate to one could be used in another. The letters to
Colonel Higginson, for example, were far more mannered than those
to her cousins Louisa[4] and Frances Norcross or her friend Mrs. J. G.
Holland, far less ardent and frightened that those to Samuel Bowles.
It was only after her father's death in 1874 that the several variant
styles began to approach a single manner. In her last years only a few
of her most intimate correspondents—the Norcrosses, Judge Lord, and
Mrs. Holland—received letters distinctly separate from a general style.

The legendary Emily Dickinson—the one about whom a number of
novels and plays and pseudo-biographies have been written—is a romantic figure. She is imagined as completely remote from the life of her
generation, a classic artist-in-a-garret (in all but the standard poverty),
unknown, unrecognized by her contemporaries. She writes because of a
hopeless love and for the same reason becomes a total recluse at an early
age.

The real Emily was just enough like the mythical to keep the legend
alive. In the last fifteen years of her life (she was fifty-five when she died)
she secluded herself from all but children, servants, doctors, immediate
family, and a few friends. But her way of life was as deliberate as her
poems and letters. Though she avoided physical contact with most of
her friends, they remained vivid envoys of the daily world, and, more
important, of the world of arts.

For a shy spinster in a small town, Emily Dickinson knew a surprising
number of notable contemporaries. Her regular correspondents, all but
a few, were known to the public of the day. Among her closest friends
were the Reverend Charles Wadsworth, sometimes considered second
only to Henry Ward Beecher (himself a friend of the family) as a pulpit
orator; Samuel Bowles, whose *Springfield Republican* had gained a na-
tional reputation; T. W. Higginson, a leading man of letters and re-
former; Helen Hunt Jackson, author of *Ramona* and (in Emerson's

---

[4] In *Letters* the name is given as Louise; Miss Norcross signed letters thus in her
later years. The Dickinsons, however, knew her as Louisa. Letters of Edward Dickinson
which speak of "Louisa" are printed in Millicent Todd Bingham's *Emily Dickinson's
Home* (New York: Harper & Row, Publishers, 1955), pp. 464, 469. Mabel Loomis
Todd, who discussed Loo with Austin and Lavinia Dickinson, and even with Frances
Norcross, used only the name Louisa. See *Letters of Emily Dickinson,* edited by Mabel
Loomis Todd (New York: Harper & Row, Publishers, 1931), pp. 214-15. (This edition
will be referred to as *Letters* [1931].)

opinion) the best poet of her time; and Josiah G. Holland, editor of *Scribner's Monthly Magazine* and best-selling novelist. The one man who indisputably returned Emily's love was Judge Otis P. Lord of the Massachusetts Supreme Court.

Many of Emily's friendships came about through the social standing of her father and brother in Amherst and the Connecticut Valley. Emily, as her sister Vinnie said, "was always watching for the rewarding person to come." [5] When one did, famous or obscure, Emily began another correspondence.

At a certain level of New England society everyone knew everyone else. So it seems, at least, to the modern student of any nineteenth-century New England writer. Among Samuel Bowles's writings one finds mention of almost all of Emily's close friends. Helen Hunt Jackson, whom Emily had first known as a child, was a protégée of Higginson, a regular writer for Holland's magazine, and a friend of Bowles.

Those correspondents who were not well-known themselves were usually close to the New England Olympus. Maria Whitney, a relative of Mrs. Samuel Bowles, was the sister of three notable men—one of them the Yale philologist William Dwight Whitney, another the geologist for whom Mount Whitney, in California, was named. Emily's aunt Catherine Sweetser had received love letters from Beecher.[6] Franklin B. Sanborn was a friend and biographer of Thoreau. Higginson's first wife was closely related to Ellery and William Ellery Channing. Mrs. Lucius Boltwood was a cousin of Emerson. Mabel Loomis Todd corresponded with Howells and the Thoreau family; her father, Eben J. Loomis (to whom Emily wrote several notes), had been a companion of Thoreau, Whitman, and Asa Gray. Emily's girlhood friend Emily Fowler was a granddaughter of Noah Webster. Even the thoroughly commonplace cousins Fanny and Louisa Norcross were friends of the sculptor Daniel Chester French, whom Emily had known slightly when he lived in Amherst.

The foregoing list (by no means complete) suggests how close even a recluse might be to the intellectual currents of her time. It explains how she could write to Higginson, "You ask me if I see any one—Judge Lord was with me a week in October, and I talked . . . once with Mr. Bowles" (II, 548). There was no need to tell which Judge Lord, which Mr. Bowles she meant. Higginson would know.

Emily Dickinson's correspondents were the only readers of the poetry she refused to publish, but she could hardly have found a more perceptive audience. Higginson and Helen Jackson shared with each other the poems and letters Emily sent them. In 1875 Higginson read and discussed some of Emily's poems in a Boston lecture on unknown poets. Mrs. Jackson memorized poems and copied them into a commonplace

---

[5] Bingham, *Emily Dickinson's Home*, p. 413.

[6] Paxton Hibben, *Henry Ward Beecher: an American Portrait* (New York: The Heritage Press, 1942), pp. 57-58.

book. She even mentioned them to her publisher, Thomas Niles of Roberts Brothers, who wrote to Emily in 1882, " 'H. H.' once told me that she wished you could be induced to publish a volume of poems. I should not want to say how highly she praised them, but to such an extent that I wish also that you could" (III, 726).

The survival of a handful of letters written to Emily Dickinson by Niles, Higginson, and Mrs. Jackson—most of them praising her poetry and asking her to publish—is still a mystery. In 1872 Emily told Louisa Norcross how she disposed of such requests: "Of Miss P—[perhaps Elizabeth Stuart Phelps, an editor of *The Woman's Journal*] I know but this, dear. She wrote me in October, requesting me to aid the world by my chirrup more. Perhaps she stated it as my duty, I don't distinctly remember, and always burn such letters, so I cannot obtain now. I replied declining" (II, 500). Just before she died, Emily asked Lavinia to burn all correspondence. Vinnie, when she carried out her sister's wish, did not read or set aside any of the letters Emily had received.[7] But on March 3, 1891, Mabel Loomis Todd wrote in her diary that Vinnie had found "a lot of letters from Col. Higginson and Helen Hunt to Emily—thank Heaven!" [8]

Probably Emily herself separated these letters from the others she had received. Since she did not order Vinnie to destroy her poems, she may have hoped that letters praising them would aid in their eventual publication. Posthumous publicity would not compromise her objection to it during her lifetime. "If fame belonged to me, I could not escape her," Emily wrote to Higginson in 1862 (II, 408). Publication then was out of the question. Editors, Emily had found, tried to smooth her off-rhymes and variable metres. She even declined to answer Helen Hunt Jackson's request to be her literary executor. That request, however, was among the letters Vinnie discovered in 1891. Perhaps, at the last, Emily tried to make sure that fame would not escape her.

In a way, her own letters were guarantees of recognition. Emily often wrote in aphorisms which transcended the daily events she was describing. The sense of royalty which she cultivated in her poems was frequent in her prose. These timeless elements have helped to keep the letters from oblivion. Even when Emily's inward royalty carried her to the brink of rudeness, her phrasing redeemed her. Mrs. Holland once made the mistake of addressing a letter to both Emily and Vinnie, and received this reply:

A mutual plum is not a plum. I was too respectful to take the pulp and do not like a stone.

[7] Millicent Todd Bingham, *Ancestors' Brocades: the Literary Debut of Emily Dickinson* (New York: Harper & Row, Publishers, 1945), pp. 26-27.

[8] *Ibid.*, p. 152.

> Send no union letters. The soul must go by Death alone, so, it must by life, if it is a soul.
> If a committee—no matter.

(II, 455)

The overstatement, understatement, and paradox which characterized Emily's poetry became part of her prose. Sometimes wit, sometimes pathos was conveyed by turning a thought inside out. In December 1881, two months after J. G. Holland died, his daughter Annie was married. Emily wrote to Mrs. Holland with paradoxical optimism, "Few daughters have the immortality of a Father for a bridal gift" (III, 720). A distraught 1861 letter to the man Emily called "Master"—probably Samuel Bowles—was an attempt to convince him of her love and pain. She began,

> Master—
> If you saw a bullet hit a Bird—and he told you he wasn't shot—you might weep at his courtesy, but you would certainly doubt his word.
> One more drop from the gash that stains your Daisy's bosom—then would you *believe?* Thomas' faith in anatomy was stronger than his faith in faith.

(II, 373)

Emily's anguish was genuine, but she could not resist a *bon mot.*

One of her favorite devices was the inclusion of poetry in the body of a letter, either in stanza form or disguised as prose. Not that all poems sent to her correspondents were made parts of the letters: the greater number of poems she gave to Higginson and to her sister-in-law Sue were enclosures on separate sheets of paper. Often, though, Emily led up to a stanza or a complete poem with a prose introduction. A love poem could become a praise of spring, for instance, by a sentence or two of preface:

> Infinite March is here, and I "hered" a bluebird! Of course I am standing on my head!
>> Go slow, my soul, to feed thyself
>> Upon his rare approach.
>> Go rapid, lest competing death
>> Prevail upon the coach.
>> Go timid, should his testing eye
>> Determine thee amiss,
>> Go boldly, for thou paidst the price,
>> Redemption for a kiss.

(II, 523)

The final stanza of another love poem, "There came a day at summer's full," took on a new meaning when adapted to the memory of a friend,

Mrs. Edward Dwight, whose picture Emily had just received from the bereaved husband:

> Again—I thank you for the face—her memory did not need—
>   Sufficient troth—that she will rise—
>   Deposed—at last—the Grave—
>   To that new fondness—Justified
>   by Calvaries of love—
>
>   (II, 389-90)

Sometimes the prose of a letter becomes merely a setting for poetry. The rough draft of an October 1870 letter to Colonel Higginson shows how much verse Emily could crowd into a single letter:

> The Riddle that we guess
> We speedily despise—
> Not anything is stale so long
> As Yesterday's Surprise—

The risks of Immortality are perhaps its' charm—A secure Delight suffers in enchantment—

The larger Haunted House it seems, of maturer Childhood—distant, an alarm—entered intimate at last as a neighbor's Cottage—

> The Spirit said unto the Dust
> Old Friend, thou knewest me
> And Time went out to tell the news
> Unto Eternity—

Those of that renown personally precious harrow like a Sunset, proved but not obtained—

Tennyson knew this, "Ah Christ—if it be possible" and even in Our Lord's "that they be with me where I am," I taste interrogation.

> Experiment escorts us last—
> His pungent company
> Will not allow an Axiom
> An Opportunity—

You speak of "tameless tastes"—A Beggar came last week—I gave him Food and Fire and as he went, "Where do you go,"

"In all the directions"—

That was what you meant

> Too happy Time dissolves itself
> And leaves no remnant by—
> 'Tis Anguish not a Feather hath
> Or too much weight to fly—
>
>   (II, 480-81)

Emily's handwriting, in her last years, was childlike and resembled widely-spaced printing rather than longhand. She wrote only two or three words to a line, so the poems she put into her letters were difficult to distinguish from her prose. Realizing this, she wrote messages which might be either. The following note, sent to Mary Warner Crowell in March 1885 as a *bon voyage* message, is a four-line stanza plus a line of prose, but the first line of the poem is separated from the others to seem a prose introduction:

> Is it too late to touch you, Dear?
>
> We this moment know—
> Love Marine and Love terrene—
> Love celestial too—
>
> I give his Angels charge—
> Emily—
> (III, 865)

George F. Whicher described such letters as Emily's game of "Guess what I am thinking." [9] There can be no doubt that she liked to mystify her correspondents. The number of puzzles depended upon the abilities of the recipient, as Emily judged them. There are few enigmas in the letters to Loo and Fanny Norcross, but a great many in messages to Higginson and Samuel Bowles.

One of Emily's strangest patterns of speech, her use of personal pronouns, seems less intentional. "Would it teach me now?" she asked Higginson in 1867 as if the Colonel were inanimate. There is the remote chance that this was the effect she intended, in order to show respect for her "preceptor," but more probably she began to write "it" or "they" instead of "you" and "he" for the sake of privacy. The first friend so impersonalized was "Master." Emily's use of this name, coupled with "Daisy" (herself), appears in the 1859 poems of Packet 1. In the same packet is this poem:

> My friend must be a Bird—
> Because it flies!
> Mortal, my friend must be,
> Because it dies!
> Barbs has it, like a Bee!
> Ah, curious friend!
> Thou puzzlest me! [10]

Not a good poem, but well enough disguised. If someone in the Dickinson household had come upon the poems of Packet 1 he would have found nothing that clearly specified a man who interested Emily.

[9] George F. Whicher, *This Was a Poet: a Critical Biography of Emily Dickinson* (New York: Charles Scribner's Sons, 1938), p. 147.
[10] *Poems*, I, 73.

The last of three surviving letter-drafts to "Master" (with deleted words and phrases in parentheses) begins, "Oh, did I offend it—(Did'nt it want me to tell it the truth) Daisy—Daisy—offend it—who bends her smaller life to his (it's) meeker every day—who only asks—a task—(who) something to do for love of it—some little way she cannot guess to make that master glad—" (II, 391). The letter dates from about 1862, and 1862 poems also make the master impersonal. But in both poetry and prose, Emily usually slipped back into the personal before she was finished. A letter-poem to Samuel Bowles, written in 1863 or 1864, begins,

> If it had no pencil
> Would it try mine—
> Worn—now—and *dull*—sweet,
> Writing much to thee.[11]

Another poem (of about 1862) is an enigmatic mixture of personal and impersonal pronouns:

> Why make it doubt—it hurts it so—
> So sick—to guess—
> So strong—to know—
> So brave—upon it's little Bed
> To tell the very last They said
> Unto Itself—and smile—and shake—
> For that dear—distant—dangerous—Sake—
> But—the Instead—the Pinching fear
> That Something—it did do—or dare—
> Offend the Vision—and it flee
> And They no more remember me—
> Nor ever turn to tell me why—
> Oh, Master. This is Misery—[12]

In this case Emily is "it," the master "They." A substitution of pronouns makes the meaning clear:

> Why make me doubt? It hurts me so—
> So sick to guess—
> So strong to know—
> So brave, upon my little bed,
> To tell the very last you said
> Unto myself, and smile and shake
> For that dear, distant, dangerous sake.

---

[11] *Ibid.*, II, 673. The catalogue of manuscripts in the Millicent Todd Bingham Collection, in the Amherst College Library, lists Bowles as the recipient of this poem.
[12] *Ibid.*, I, 356-57.

> But the Instead—the pinching fear
> That something I did do or dare
> Offend the vision, and it flee
> And you no more remember me,
> Nor ever turn to tell me why—
> Oh, Master, this is misery!

Emily was aware of the strange effect she was creating in such poems. An 1862 poem begins, in its draft form,

> While "it" is alive—
> Until Death—touches it—
> While "it" and I—lap one—Air—[13]

as if the poet could not decide whether to set off the unusual pronoun by quotation marks. In the final copy of the poem there are none.

Many of Emily Dickinson's 1862-64 poems employ "it" or "this" to refer to death, perhaps as an extension of the theme of death which runs through so many poems about the dangerously ill "Master." After 1864 the peculiar pronouns diminished. Emily called Colonel Higginson "it" in 1867, but did not repeat the word in a personal sense until December 1878, when she congratulated him on his engagement to Mary P. Thacher: "Till it has loved—no man or woman can become itself—" (II, 628). Here the problem seems to be grammatical. The construction demanded the singular pronoun, but "he" or "she," "himself" or "herself" would have been inappropriate.

Meanwhile another circumlocution had appeared in Emily's letters. She was peculiarly sensitive to the words "wife" and "husband," and often found ways to avoid them. The series of marriage poems she wrote between 1860 and 1863 establish the special meaning of the words:

> I'm "wife"—I've finished that—
> That other state—
> I'm Czar—I'm "Woman" now— . . .[14]
>
> "My Husband"—women say—
> Stroking the melody— . . .
>
> (II, 758)

Emily began to avoid the words when she spoke of others' marriages. Like her impersonal pronouns, her oblique references to marriage were sporadic. When she spoke of the first Mrs. Higginson in the letters of

[13] *Ibid.*, I, 374.
[14] *Ibid.*, I, 142.

1876-78 she sometimes wrote "Mrs. Higginson," sometimes "your friend."
In November 1878 she was able to write, "I had a sweet Forenoon with
Mrs. Jackson recently, who brought her Husband to me for the first
time— . . ." (II, 627), but Mr. Jackson was not always so described.
Helen Hunt Jackson quoted one of the circumlocutions in an 1879 letter
to Emily: " 'The man I live with' (I suppose you recollect designating
my husband by that curiously direct phrase) is in New York— . . ." (II,
639).

Colonel Higginson and Mrs. Jackson were amused by such oddities of
speech. Yet obliquities also occur in Lavinia Dickinson's letters. When
Mabel Loomis Todd was away from Amherst in the spring of 1883,
Vinnie wrote to her about Professor Todd: "I've seen your companion
once. I should be glad to lessen his loneliness in any way in my
power." [15] Either the sisters habitually avoided speaking directly of marriage, or Emily's substitute words crept into Vinnie's vocabulary.

Other oddities of the Dickinson prose style include archaisms and
localisms. Emily's capitalization of words within the sentence may be
called archaic, but it is not a problem of style, nor (usually) are the
short dashes she used as a rhythmic device or in lieu of punctuation.
More fundamental are her Elizabethan turns of speech, probably gained
through her intimate knowledge of the King James Bible and Shakespeare. When Emily writes "What Miracles the News is!" (II, 483) one
is reminded of Shakespearean constructions like "All is but toys." [16]
There is the flavor of Shakespeare, too, in a comment on a dead child:,
"The little Furniture of Loss has Lips of Dirks to stab us" (III, 679).

Emily's subjunctive was another archaism. Coupled with the New
England colloquial substitution of "be" for "is," it appeared often in
her poetry, occasionally in her prose. When the old-fashioned form
appears in a letter, there is a good chance that a poem is present, disguised as prose. "That you be with me annuls fear" (II, 482) is strictly
prose, but the following sentences makes a poem: "Too few the morn-
ings be, too scant the nights. No lodging can be had for the delights
that come to earth to stay, but no apartment find and ride away" (II,
488).

Regionalisms are most frequent in Emily's girlhood letters,[17] though
she wrote "a'nt" (for "isn't"), "he don't," and "eno' " when she was mature. Like her subjunctives, most of her localisms made her writing terser.
One of the few exceptions is the added "that" in "because that you were
coming" (II, 402) or "because that he would die" (II, 431). Occasionally
Emily's expressions may mislead the modern reader. For instance, a poem
sent to the Bowleses after the birth of a son in 1861 hopes that when
the baby begins to talk, his scriptural "Forbid us not—" will sound

---

[15] Bingham, *Ancestors' Brocades*, p. 8.
[16] *Macbeth*, II, 99.
[17] See Whicher, *This Was a Poet*, p. 232.

"Some like 'Emily' ": *somewhat* like "Emily." [18] The conditional "did you not" for "if you did not" has misled many editors of "The Snake."

The uniqueness of Emily Dickinson's prose style does not depend on these minor oddities of diction. Rather, it lies in her originality of thought and her ability to set down her ideas in prose almost as compact and dramatic as her poetry. Emily pared all that seemed superfluous, even usual connectives, from the essence of her thought.

The letters Emily wrote were part of her art, but the life she chose made them also her conversation and autobiography. Her prose tells a great deal about her poetry, simply because the same mind conceived both in much the same way. The letters point the way toward art before Emily wrote a line of passable verse, and the last words she wrote were those of a letter. Now that more than a thousand of her letters are in print it is possible to follow with some accuracy the course of Emily's life in her prose expressions of it, and in the letter-poems she sent to friends. There are still gaps—some as long as a year—but the real Emily Dickinson, far more interesting than the legendary one, has begun to emerge from generations of myth and misconception.

[18] *Poems*, III, 875.

Chronology of Important Dates

1830, December 10	Born in Amherst, Mass.
1840	Enters Amherst Academy (graduated 1847).
1844, May-June	Visits relatives in Boston, Cambridge, Worcester.

Other visits outside Amherst:

1851—her brother Austin in Boston, Mass.

1853, autumn—the Hollands in Springfield, Mass.

1854 (?), 1855 (?), winter—Washington, D.C. and Philadelphia.

1861, October—Middletown, Conn.

1864, February, November—Boston, for eye treatment.

1865, April, October (?)—Boston, for eye treatment.

1847-8	Attends Mt. Holyoke Female Seminary, South Hadley, Mass.
1850, February	Valentine to George Gould, "Awake ye muses nine, sing me a strain divine," published, Amherst College *Indicator*.

Other poems published during her lifetime:

1852, February 20—" 'Sic transit gloria mundi,' " *Springfield Daily Republican*.

1861, May 4—"I taste a liquor never brewed," *Springfield Daily Republican*.

1862, March 1—"Safe in their Alabaster Chambers," *Springfield Daily Republican*.

1864, March 12—"Some keep the Sabbath going to Church," *The Round Table*.

1864, March 30—"Blazing in Gold and quenching in Purple," *Springfield Daily Republican*.

1866, February 14—"A narrow Fellow in the Grass," *Springfield Daily Republican*. 1878, "Success is counted sweetest," *A Masque of Poets,* Boston.

1857, December 16	R. W. Emerson lectures in Amherst, visits the Austin Dickinsons.
1862, April 15	First letter to Thomas Wentworth Higginson asking for literary advice.
1870, August 17	T. W. Higginson visits ED in Amherst.
1873, December 3	T. W. Higginson makes a second and final visit.
1874, June 16	ED's father, Edward Dickinson, dies in Boston.
1876, August 20	Helen Hunt Jackson asks ED to contribute to *A Masque of Poets*.
1878, July 25	Article in *Springfield Daily Republican* suggests ED as collaborator on the "Saxe Holm" stories with Helen Hunt Jackson.

1882, November 14	Mrs. Edward Dickinson dies.
1883, March 31	Thomas Niles asks ED to submit a volume of poems for publication.
1886, May 15	Dies in Amherst.
1890	*Poems by Emily Dickinson,* First Series, ed. by Mabel Loomis Todd and T. W. Higginson.
1891	*Poems by Emily Dickinson,* Second Series, ed. by T. W. Higginson and Mabel Loomis Todd.
1894	*Letters of Emily Dickinson* ed. by Mabel Loomis Todd.
1896	*Poems by Emily Dickinson,* Third Series, ed. by Mabel Loomis Todd.
1914	*The Single Hound* ed. by Martha Dickinson Bianchi.
1924	*The Life and Letters of Emily Dickinson* ed. by Martha Dickinson Bianchi. *The Complete Poems of Emily Dickinson* ed. by Martha Dickinson Bianchi and Alfred Leete Hampson.
1929	*Further Poems of Emily Dickinson* ed. by Martha Dickinson Bianchi.
1931	*Letters of Emily Dickinson* ed. by Mabel Loomis Todd.
1932	*Emily Dickinson Face to Face: Unpublished Letters with Notes and Reminiscences* by Martha Dickinson Bianchi.
1935	*Unpublished Poems of Emily Dickinson* ed. by Martha Dickinson Bianchi and Alfred Leete Hampson.
1937	*Poems by Emily Dickinson* ed. by Martha Dickinson Bianchi and Alfred Leete Hampson.
1945	*Bolts of Melody: New Poems of Emily Dickinson* ed. by Mabel Loomis Todd and Millicent Todd Bingham.
1951	*Emily Dickinson's Letters to Dr. and Mrs. Josiah Gilbert Holland* ed. by Theodora Van Wagenen Ward.
1955	*The Poems of Emily Dickinson,* 3 vols., "Including variant readings critically compared with all known manuscripts," ed. by Thomas H. Johnson.
1958	*The Letters of Emily Dickinson,* 3 vols., ed. by Thomas H. Johnson and Theodora Ward.

Notes on the Editor and Authors

RICHARD B. SEWALL is Professor of English and Master of Ezra Stiles College at Yale University. He is the author of *The Vision of Tragedy*, and is currently at work on a life of Emily Dickinson.

CONRAD AIKEN is the author of *Collected Poems, Collected Short Stories*, and *A Reviewer's ABC: Collected Criticism*.

CHARLES R. ANDERSON is Professor of American Literature at Johns Hopkins University. He is the author of *Emily Dickinson's Poetry: Stairway of Surprise, Melville in the South Seas*, and editor of the *Centennial Edition of Sidney Lanier*.

R. P. BLACKMUR is Professor of English at Princeton University. He is the author of *Language as Gesture, Form and Value in Modern Poetry*, and *The Lion and the Honeycomb*.

LOUISE BOGAN, poet and critic, is the author of *Achievement in American Poetry* and *Selected Criticism*.

DAVID J. M. HIGGINS' essay is the first chapter of his Ph.D. thesis, *Portrait of Emily Dickinson: The Poet and Her Prose*, written for the Faculty of Philosophy at Columbia University. He is an Instructor in English at Rutgers State University.

THOMAS H. JOHNSON is Chairman of the English Department at Lawrenceville. He is the author of *Emily Dickinson, An Interpretive Biography* and editor of *The Poems of Emily Dickinson* and *The Letters of Emily Dickinson*.

ARCHIBALD MacLEISH, poet, playwright, and critic, holds the Boylston professorship at Harvard.

JOHN CROWE RANSOM is a Senior Fellow of the Indiana University School of Letters. He is the author of several books of poems and many critical essays.

JAMES REEVES is a free-lance English author and broadcaster. His publications include *Collected Poems* and *A Short History of English Poetry*.

ALLEN TATE, novelist, critic, and poet, is Professor of English at the University of Minnesota.

DONALD E. THACKREY's essay is the second chapter of his book, *Emily Dickinson's Approach to Poetry*. Mr. Thackrey is Editor of Publications, Office of Research Administration, University of Michigan.

AUSTIN WARREN is Professor of English at the University of Michigan. He is the author of *Rage for Order* and, with René Wellek, *Theory of Literature*.

HENRY W. WELLS, Associate Professor of English at Columbia University, is the author of *Poet and Psychiatrist: Merrill Moore* and *Poetic Imagery, Illustrated from Elizabethan Literature*.

GEORGE F. WHICHER, author of *This Was a Poet: A Critical Biography of Emily Dickinson,* also edited *Poetry of the New England Renaissance, 1790-1890.*

RICHARD WILBUR is Professor of English at Wesleyan University. His books of poems include *Ceremony and Other Poems, Things of This World,* and *Advice to a Prophet and Other Poems.*

YVOR WINTERS, poet and critic, is Professor of English at Stanford University. In criticism, he is the author of *In Defense of Reason* and *The Poetry of W. B. Yeats.*

Selected Bibliography

THE POEMS AND LETTERS

Johnson, Thomas H., ed., *The Poems of Emily Dickinson*, "Including variant readings critically compared with all known manuscripts," 3 vols. (Cambridge, Mass.: The Belknap Press of Harvard University Press), 1955.

Johnson, Thomas H., ed., *The Complete Poems of Emily Dickinson* (Boston: Little, Brown & Co.), 1960. The text of the 3-vol. edition, with the variant readings omitted.

Johnson, Thomas H., and Theodora Ward, eds., *The Letters of Emily Dickinson*, 3 vols. (Cambridge, Mass.: The Belknap Press of Harvard University Press), 1958.

BOOKS

(In addition to those represented in this anthology.)

Bingham, Millicent Todd, *Ancestors' Brocades, The Literary Debut of Emily Dickinson* (New York: Harper & Row, Publishers), 1945; *Emily Dickinson, A Revelation* (New York: Harper & Row, Publishers), 1954; *Emily Dickinson's Home* (New York: Harper & Row, Publishers), 1955.

Chase, Richard, *Emily Dickinson* (New York: William Sloane Associates, Inc.), 1951.

Leyda, Jay, *The Years and Hours of Emily Dickinson* (New Haven: Yale University Press), 1960.

Patterson, Rebecca, *The Riddle of Emily Dickinson* (Boston and New York: Houghton Mifflin Company), 1951.

Ward, Theodora, *The Capsule of the Mind: Chapters in the Life of Emily Dickinson* (Cambridge, Mass.: The Belknap Press of Harvard University Press), 1961.

BIBLIOGRAPHIES

Hampson, Alfred Leete, *Emily Dickinson, A Bibliography* (Northampton: The Hampshire Bookshop), 1930.

Emily Dickinson, A Bibliography, with a Foreword by George F. Whicher (Amherst: The Jones Library, Inc.), 1930.

TWENTIETH CENTURY VIEWS

Forthcoming Titles

EMILY DICKINSON
(THE TWENTIETH CENTURY VIEWS SERIES)

Edited by RICHARD B. SEWALL

OUT OF THE MISTS of sentiment and legend which long obscured her real identity and power, a new Emily Dickinson is emerging, thanks to the careful work of editors, scholars, and critics—especially since the publication of the Harvard variorum edition of her complete poems in 1955.

The theme of the present volume is set by the title of one of its pivotal essays, "A Poet Restored," by John Crowe Ransom. Ransom and his fellow critics help us see why Emily Dickinson is not only a great woman poet and a great American poet but, to quote Yvor Winters, ". . . except by Melville, she is surpassed by no writer that this country has produced; she is one of the greatest lyric poets of all time."

Selections in this volume include:

Emily Dickinson ALLEN TATE

Sumptuous Destitution
  RICHARD WILBUR

(Continued on back flap)